3⁵⁰

underlined
196 p.
1968

The Missionary Between the Times

THE MISSIONARY
BETWEEN
THE TIMES

R. Pierce Beaver

DOUBLEDAY & COMPANY, INC., GARDEN CITY, NEW YORK

1968

Foreword

The present pace of radical change is altering our perspective on time. More important differences appear in a decade now than formerly in a century. We have been accustomed to divide history into ancient, medieval, and modern periods. However, a new global society with a single world history is so rapidly emerging that all previous experience of our race may perhaps now be regarded as ancient. Urban-industrial-scientific man with his secular world view and values, technological developments, the interrelation of peoples, the population explosion, and space exploration are giving humanity a new face and a new world in which to live. A dozen separate revolutions are taking place within a huge one that includes them all. Yet through all the change human nature seems to alter very little.

The Church's mission and the missionary are caught in

the confusion, uncertainties, and perplexities of these revolutionary changes. That mission goes on until the "End," but its forms and ways must be radically modified to meet the challenge of the revolution. No fixed chart or blueprint can at present be laid out for the future. But some word can be spoken to the missionary and the membership of the Church as they stand at this moment between the times. And this scrutiny of the missionary situation may bring some illumination and understanding to the general public regarding the present state of that tremendous force in international and intercultural relations recently discovered by the general historians. Involvement now takes different forms than in the nineteenth century, but the Christian world mission with its hundred thousand agents in the nations of the "Third World" is still a mighty significant factor in international affairs and cultural exchange.

This book grew out of lectures given to newly appointed and furloughed missionaries, to members of mission boards, and to conference audiences of laymen and ministers during the last few years. It has taken final shape through lectures given during the academic years 1965–66 and 1966–67, especially at the Lutheran School of Theology's School of Missions at Chicago, Luther Theological Seminary at St. Paul, and Concordia Seminary in St. Louis. Those who heard or read the lectures have been kind to say that they bring information and perspectives sought by mission board executives and directors, pastors, churchmen, and the general public who are concerned for the welfare of, or skeptical about, the future of the mission enterprise.

The form and content show that this book was produced for Americans, but, since there is only one world mission, the whole of it has been kept in view. Roman

Catholic friends say that excepting for organizational factors the plight of the Roman Catholic missionary is about
the same as that of the Protestant portrayed here. The
British factor, and more especially the influence of the
Church Missionary Society, is clearly evident. Principles
apply as much to the new missionaries of Asian churches
as to Americans. It is the Christian missionary, whatever
his denomination or nation, with whom we are concerned.

The manuscript has been read by a number of friends
whose comments were helpful, especially Professor William J. Danker of Concordia Seminary, Dr. Alford Carle-
ton, Executive Vice-President of the United Church Board
for World Ministries, and the Rev. Paul R. Gregory, Pacific
area secretary of the same board. Grateful acknowledgment is made of permission to quote from books as follows: The SCM Press, London, for a passage by Lesslie
Newbigin in *The Missionary Church in East and West*,
edited by Charles C. West and David M. Paton; Lutterworth Press, London, Westminster Press, Philadelphia, for
a quotation from *Missions in a Time of Testing* by Ronald
K. Orchard; and Hodder and Stoughton, Ltd., London, for
passages from *The Making of a Missionary* by Douglas N.
Sargent.

Contents

CONTENTS   xiii

The Missionary Between the Times

I

Why Send Missionaries?

Why send missionaries? They have been expelled from the Sudan, Burma, China, and parts of Assam in India. Their entrance is severely restricted in Indonesia and some other countries. Why then do churches persist in sending missionaries? Some nationalists in new countries say that missionaries are sent to be subversive agents of Western imperialist nations. Some Christians in those same countries suspect that missionaries are sent to perpetuate foreign control of the national churches. When asked this question some American churchmen, honestly perplexed, can only ask in reply: "Why should we send them?" Recent book titles reflect the big question mark raised today over the missionary's right to be: *The Unpopular Missionary, The Ugly Missionary,* and *Missionary, Go Home!*[1]

Such questioning of the propriety of sending missionaries is not new. It has been raised again and again ever since the time of the Reformation. Yet never since mission was generally accepted by the churches early in the nineteenth century has its justification been so widely challenged as at present. American churchmen give more money for mission today than ever before, but personal commitment and participation are at an extremely low ebb. The question is being raised most insistently: Why send missionaries? The answer is simply that this is the Church's real business. It cannot be the Church unless it *sends* witnesses to God's action in Christ as well as makes witness to the gospel where it is established.

The Apostolate

The Church exists primarily for its apostolate. This central and basic function of the spiritual-human organism known as the body of Christ can be called making witness, proclamation of the gospel, mission, or evangelism. These words are frequently used with identical meaning, but again are often employed with distinction. They can all be comprehended within the term apostolate.

The words apostle, apostolic, and apostolate come from a Greek root having the idea of the sending of a messenger with a special task or message set by the sender. Apostle in the New Testament denotes a man sent directly with the full authority of Christ or as the commissioned representative of a congregation of believers. The Twelve Apostles got official office in the Church because they were sharers in a more general apostolate of the whole company of disciples and were also in a very special way witnesses of the death and resurrection of our Lord and had been personally chosen by Him as authoritative bearers of His message. Paul, far more than any of the Twelve, is the model of the Christian apostle. Apostleship was the gift of the risen Lord to the whole Church, His commissioning of His people to the privilege and duty of caring for the salvation of the nations in His name. The gift of the Pentecostal power, of the Holy Spirit for effective witnessing, came down upon the entire company of disciples gathered together with one accord. The discharge of this apostolate is the Church's first task between the Ascension and the culmination of history symbolically called the End.

All other functions of the Church are subordinate to apostolate and support it. Thus that extremely important function, worship, is the celebration of faith before the eyes of mankind and a proclamation of that faith before all people. The Lord's Supper or Eucharist, which is at the very heart of worship, is the primary means by which the members become one in their Lord, the Eucharistic Bread, to be broken with Him for His healing of the nations.

St. Paul calls the apostolate the ministry or service of reconciliation through which the message of reconciliation is proclaimed. That message in essence is compressed by the Fourth Gospel into one sentence: "For God so loved the world that he gave his only Son, that whoever believes in him should not perish but have eternal life" (John 3:16). Paul states the responsibility of the Church and all its members with respect to this gospel or good news. He writes: "All this is from God, who through Christ reconciled us to himself and gave us the ministry of reconciliation; that is, God was in Christ reconciling the world to himself, not counting their trespasses against them, and entrusting to us the message of reconciliation. So we are ambassadors for Christ, God making his appeal through us" (2 Cor. 5:18–20). It is for faithfulness in this work that God has put the Church into the world and given it an essential role in the grand consummation of history under divine providence.

The New Testament reveals the sensitive consciousness of the early disciples to their apostolic vocation. They recognized the voice of the risen Lord among them commanding: "Go therefore and make disciples of all nations"; "you shall receive power when the Holy Spirit has come upon you; and you shall be my witnesses in Jerusalem and in all Judea and in Samaria and to the end of the earth" (Matt. 28:19; Acts 1:8). Even without this conviction about direct sending, those first Christians would have known that the Church was sent into the world by Jesus Christ just as He had been sent by the Father. There is command to apostolic service in the injunction, "Take up [your] cross and follow me" (Matt. 16:24; Mark 8:34; Luke 9:23). When two or three gathered together in the name of Jesus, His presence and the impulse of the Holy Spirit sent them forth to testify to men near and far. Worship ended in proclamation—or the worshipful life continued in proclamation. St. Paul taught that in the celebration of the Eucharist the disciples participate in Christ, and participation means sharing His mission (1 Cor. 10:16–21). Showing both in their worship and in their common life that the Church is the first fruit of the Kingdom of God or the token fellowship of the New Age, the people of Christ went out from the holy table to be heralds of that Kingdom and its King. It was through this participation in its Lord and Head that the Church soon got its characteristics of being "one, holy, catholic, and apostolic." The body of Christ was knit together in a unity which convinced men that God actually does reconcile men with Himself and with one another in Christ (John 17:21). It was not separation from a dirty world which made it holy, but, on the contrary, its going out into that world in

Christ's mission of healing and redemption. It manifested its inherent catholicity as it gathered more and more diverse and separated peoples into the universal fold of the one Shepherd. It was inherently apostolic by nature, but it manifested this character, not by being ruled and getting authority from the Twelve, but by spending the common and individual lives in proclamation.

There were missionaries called apostles long after the last of the Twelve Apostles died. Hosts of laymen for many generations exercised their apostolic ministry, telling the good news, founding churches far and wide. The title apostle was rarely used in later centuries, but it was applied to great pioneer missionaries, such as Ulfilas, Apostle to the Goths (d. ca. 380), and Francis Xavier, Apostle to the Indies (1506–1552). John Calvin affirmed that throughout the centuries and in his own time God had now and then raised up apostles, "missionaries who were to reduce the world from their revolt to true obedience to God, and to establish his Kingdom universally by the proclaiming of the gospel."[2] The Moravians applied the title and adjective to evangelistic missionaries in the eighteenth century. Despite the general loss of zeal in the Church at large over many centuries, there were always some missionaries sent as apostles to the nations, even when there was little real concern for local evangelism and persons were just born into the Church because they saw the light of day within Christendom and were automatically eligible for baptism. The founding of the Sacred Congregation for the Propagation of the Faith in the seventeenth century by the Church of Rome and of official mission boards by Protestant churches in the nineteenth century theoretically restored the apostolate to centrality, but practice has never matched profession. The Church of Rome has long used the word apostolate for special types of Christian action, such as "the lay apostolate," but it was only after the end of World War II that it became common among European Protestants. More recently it has been introduced into American usage. The word may not be properly used, however, unless it includes the dimension of *sending.*

Suddenly today there has become current a theological awareness of the basic place of the apostolate in the life of the Church. Substantial theological and biblical studies of mission are more numerous than in the entire previous course of church history. Vatican Council II clearly affirmed the obligation of "the pilgrim church . . . missionary by her very nature" to carry the gospel to every creature.[3] The merger of the International Missionary Council with the World Council of Churches at New Delhi in 1961 was theoretically an affirmation by the member denominations of the missionary nature of the Church. Denominational and ecumenical documents in profusion set forth the centrality of the encounter of the gospel with the world through the action of the servant Church. The *Affirmations on God's Mission* adopted by the Lutheran Church–Missouri Synod, for example, if taken seriously by pastors and people would revolutionize parish and denominational life and ministry. They have taken a giant step in creating a new denominational administrative order for mission action. Can the implications be carried both into the functioning of that new order and to the very grass roots of that denomination's life? The present stress on the witness of the laity, proposals for "Joint Action for Mission," the "Wheaton Declaration,"[4] and the new American preoccupation with ministry in urban industrial secular society all attest to the recovery of an awareness of apostolate. The extensive international study on "The Missionary Structure of

the Congregation" carries this concern down to the most
elemental form of Christian community on the local
level.[5] The Commission on World Mission and Evangelism at its Mexico meeting declared: "We therefore affirm
that this missionary movement now involves Christians
on all six continents and in all lands. It must be the
common witness of the whole Church bringing the whole
gospel to the whole world."[6]

All this mass of literature makes it appear as if in our
day the Church has suddenly and wholeheartedly recognized its apostolic nature and purpose. Unfortunately,
however, there is a tremendous gap between the perspective of the scholar and that of pulpit and pew, between
insight and action. It is true that a very active minority
does now indeed have a passionate devotion to apostolate.
But it is ironical that under the slogan "one world mission" concern should be so overwhelmingly about Christians confronting that world only in the society where
they are residents and citizens. One world mission is acknowledged, but yet the question is asked: Why send
missionaries? Encounter with the world just where the
Church exists and Christians abound is only half the apostolate. It is the lesson of history, as this writer reads it,
that when sending is neglected the wellsprings of evangelism dry up.

Bishop Douglas N. Sargent reminds us that in dealing
with the question "Who wants missionaries?" we must begin and end with asking what God wants. Does He want
missionaries? The answer is an emphatic YES![7] Christ's
command to preach the gospel to every creature comes
to us in the context of the entire New Testament and
record of the early Church. To attempt to limit the effectiveness of Christ's death to us and our near neighbors
is to reduce it to meaninglessness. God has called all peo-

ples to Him in Christ, and inherent in that calling is God's GO to the Church. Father Dournes went to the obscure Jarai tribe in the mountains of Vietnam because "the Jarai too were *called*"; and just as God makes the first move to come to us, so the Church in the persons of sent representatives goes to people who do not answer because they have not heard the call.[8]

The Theological Imperative

Here it is possible only to hint at the biblical and theological foundations of the Church's apostolate. It is part of the creative, revelatory, and redemptive work of God Himself. God never ceases creating. The Church in apostolic service is an agent which He employs. On the one hand, when an estranged sinful man accepts the message of salvation brought to him in the ministry of reconciliation and turns to God in Christ with faith "he is a new creation; the old has passed away, behold, the new has come" (2 Cor. 5:17). On the other hand, it was also the expectation of the New Testament Church that this ministry of reconciliation would be used by God toward the transformation of the whole of humanity under the lordship of Christ, to the coming of what may be called a new heaven and earth, to the establishment of God's will in this world, resulting in a new society in a universe transformed and harmonized with its Creator. Both of these are works of creation, and God uses the Church and its member disciples to effect them.

Moreover, the Church in mission is the bearer of God's revelation. The Holy Spirit, the Illuminator, the Lord and Giver of Life in the terms of the Creed, the great Missionary, both goes before and accompanies the

ambassador of the cross of Christ. Because God has already given men everywhere some knowledge of His truth
through general revelation in nature, cultural traditions,
and religion, many Christians, from the time of the writer
of the Fourth Gospel, have believed that Christ as
Logos Spermaticos, the divine life-giving Word, has been
present with all men as Truth and Light and that all men
are potentially members in His body. Thus Father Rai-
mundo Pannikar can speak of the Hidden Christ of Hinduism—or of Buddhism or of Confucianism; Karl Rahner
and Edward C. F. A. Schillebeeckx can talk of "anonymous Christians," and Paul Tillich of "the latent Church."
Furthermore, God is with every man, His child, in the
revolutionary circumstances of his society today, in his
family, and in his inner consciousness. Where God and
Christ are, there is the Holy Spirit too. The missionary
or evangelist never announces the gospel without some
preparation having been made for that proclamation both
in the past dealing of God with the people and in the
present encounter. The Spirit of God is there at work. It
is He who brings the illumination that awakens faith. Only
the Holy Spirit can bring a man to call Christ Lord. Belief awaits hearing; hearing awaits a preacher; and the
preacher must be sent (Rom. 10:14–15). But the Holy
Spirit has been sent ahead of him. When the gospel is
proclaimed to a person or a people and there is a positive
response, the new knowledge and understanding is as
much a fresh revelation of God's truth as when first
spoken by the mouth of Jesus or of St. Paul.

Moreover, the apostolate is clearly an agency of God's
redeeming work. It is the word and deed of God's love
among men mediated by a messenger-servant who has
himself known that love. God has always sought wayward
and rebellious men before they have turned to Him. He

called Abraham and chose Israel to be a beacon of saving
light to the nations. He acted in the vast sending mission
of Judaism in the intertestamental and early Church periods. He sent His Son to make the Father's nature and
will known and to draw all men to the Divine Parent in
reconciled unity. Jesus chose the Apostles and sent out disciples on trial missions. The Son and the Holy Spirit sent
the Church, the continuing body of Christ, to announce
salvation and to be the voice, hands, and feet of our Lord
in the healing of the nations. There is no nation, no single
unreconciled man, who is not the object of the divine
sending.

The Church's mission is first of all Christ's own mission, revealing truth, applying it to life, teaching, feeding,
healing, liberating, loving even to the cost of death as
Jesus did in the flesh. But the Church has its own mission,
too, and that is to proclaim who Jesus Christ is and what
God has done through Him: that He is Saviour, Reconciler,
Lord; the Way, Truth, and Life; the Good Shepherd, the
Great Physician, Prince of Peace, Whom men must know,
love, and believe in for present and eternal salvation. It
gathers those whom the Holy Spirit has caused to call
Christ Lord into the fold of the Shepherd and the body
of Christ, making them partners in their Lord in His mission. Yes, the mission or apostolate is *missio Dei*, the
mission of God—Father, Son, and Holy Spirit; but God
sent the Church to be the body of Christ in saving service, and there is no mission in and to the world apart from
the devotion, initiative, and perseverance of Christ's disciples. The mission is as fully human as it is divine.

The word of God is proclaimed through the apostolate
in three forms. The first is the verbal word, spoken and
printed. The message must be communicated. As Eugene
A. Nida has well emphasized, God's word is put into

man's language, linguistically and culturally, so that it can be understood when heard. A century and a half ago our forefathers called oral preaching the "grand means" of mission. The word spoken by the living ambassador of the Cross with contagious conviction remains indispensable. Yet this writer finds more and more Africans and Asians who say that while the message is intrinsically good it is unconvincing. They claim that the lives, attitudes, and actions of professed Christians—even missionaries and evangelists—run contrary to it.

The spoken message needs must be matched by the dramatic word of loving service without thought of self or profit by which the compassion and mercy of God are spoken in deeds by the servant-friends of our Lord. Teaching, healing, feeding the hungry, relieving need and suffering, bringing aids and skills for more abundant physical existence and emotional and spiritual health, efforts for social justice and human rights—all these activities have been used as bait to catch hearers. But when rightly done purely out of Christ's own love for His brethren they can have no ulterior aim. They are God's love in Christ through His disciples speaking to the loveless and the unloved, that is, the unloved by the world. Freely given love meeting human need can be effective preaching of the gospel, the word in action which validates the spoken word and spreads faith by contagion.

Thirdly, the word spoken and that declared in service get their ultimate authenticity in the eyes of skeptical hearers and beholders from the word made manifest in Christian unity. The actual demonstration of love in unity in the Christian family is most convincing. The writer has often heard from Asians and Africans the assertion that the scandal of disunity, unbrotherliness, and internecine strife robs the spoken word of power. People of new nations seeking unity and stability fear what they believe to be the inherent divisiveness of Christianity. If God has indeed reconciled the world to Himself in Jesus Christ, the vertical union of men with God in Christ ought to be made manifest in the horizontal union of Christian disciples with one another—one in their Lord despite human diversities, bearing one another's burdens in forgiveness and mutual helpfulness. St. John's Gospel reports our Lord's prayer "that they may all be one; as thou, Father, art in me, and I in thee, that they also may be one in us: *that the world may believe that thou hast sent me.*" Reconciliation demonstrated in mutual love and care is the most convincing word that can be preached to non-believers.

The apostolate is simultaneously directed to "Jerusalem and the end of the earth"—to every man and to all nations. Each and every disciple by his baptism or profession of faith is ordained an evangelist, and some are sent forth on behalf of all. John Wesley declared: "The world is my parish." The world is, in some sense, the field of witness of every Christian in his own place and through his sent representatives. There are two parts of the apostolate which together make up one inseparable whole. Neither may be neglected. I will call them here *evangelism* and *sending*.

These two words are popularly confused. Sending is mission, and the word mission is now being used to cover every aspect of the encounter of the gospel with the world. The word evangelism has in America and to some extent in Europe long been demoted from its original meaning of proclamation of the evangel, and has been applied mostly to cultivating the recommitment of nominal or lapsed Christians, and it has even degenerated into promotion of church membership.[9] Recent studies and the search for new forms of ministry are restoring the true meaning of the term. Actually, both mission, or sending, and evangelism can be used to designate the whole of the apostolate, but distinction between local witness and witness to the nations through sending must be made. Therefore I use these words with meanings which will become clear in the following paragraphs. The reader may substitute words which may seem to him better choices.

Evangelism or Local Witness

Evangelism, as used here, is witness to Christ's saviourhood and lordship through the ministry of reconciliation where each congregation worships and enjoys fellowship and where each disciple member earns his daily bread and supports his family. Such witness is made in worship, preaching, and teaching in the house of God. The fellowship and mutual caring of the members of the local church should be such as to show forth the reality of reconciliation. Mutual forgiveness and concern ought to be evident. Evangelism includes the word spoken in testimony to friends, neighbors, and all persons encountered in the course of the day's business and pleasure. Witness may be made in the discharge of Christian vocation in business, craft, or profession. It should be effected also through the visible quality of the home, which is the Church in microcosm. It should be made through active community ministry by the congregation in service to nonmembers in all their needs and suffering. It includes the stand which the congregation makes on social issues in seeking liberation, justice, rights, and opportunities for others and the demonstration of the relevance of the gospel to those matters. Despite the criticisms leveled today against the traditional parish structure, every congregation can do these things. But evangelism should call forth new forms of the local church now evidently needed in our new urban industrial secularized society. Store-front churches, coffeehouses, cells or fellowship groups meeting in homes of believers represent efforts to find such forms. All the local churches in a given community, region, or nation should seek to make united witness together. The Evangelism-in-Depth campaigns in Latin American countries initiated and sponsored by the Latin America Mission are achieving such cooperation and united action.[10]

American "home missions" have been and still are too much a kind of denominational imperialist church extension program. Yet increasingly during the past half-century there has been growing concern for genuine evangelism. Laymen are being called to witness and ministry. Resources are pooled by the several churches in united special ministries to migrant workers, hospital patients, visitors to national parks, deprived minorities, and the people of blighted, poverty-stricken areas. The present passion for ministry in the inner city, the effort to make an impact on contemporary secular society, the involvement in the struggle for justice and human rights, the agonizing over intelligible language and worship, the search for new forms of Christian assembly and ministry, the emergence of such organs as the Urban Training Center for Christian Mission in Chicago all reveal clearly the extent of the present engagement in one half of the apostolate. This is what "world mission" now means to most personally concerned and committed American churchmen. The vigorous effort by the World Student Christian Movement to popularize the idea of "Christian presence" is a token of this universal concern in many lands.

Mission or Sending

Nevertheless, there is another half of the apostolate which dare not be neglected or subordinated. This is the sending, that is, mission in its more traditional sense. It is the evangelistic outreach beyond the home locality, involving the commissioning and sending of a representative agent, the missionary. He makes witness and gives service on behalf of the sending church and its disciples. This is how the church members become Christ's witnesses in Samaria and at the end of the earth as well as in Jerusalem and Judea. The distance in miles or kilometers which the missionary travels to his place of ministry is not significant. It may even be within his own country. However, be it near or far, that missionary must go to some people who dwell in what is to him a distant "end of the earth," a people far off and alien to the sending church. Much is now made of the disappearance of the geographical ends of the earth in a time of jet travel, instantaneous communications, and international interdependence and when there is a Christian community of some size in almost every nation. Nevertheless *ends* remain; and sociological, cultural, religious, and ideological "far ends of the earth" may be discovered in profusion. The groups engaged in the World Council of Churches' present "Study of the Missionary Structure of the Congregation" have tended to turn it into a "Study of New Structures for Mission," and have played down "missionary" in favor of engagement with the world where each church is. They tend to define mission as discharge of the apostolate anywhere, and to stress "sociological multiplicities" over against "geographical multiplicities." Consequently, the study has become largely a most welcome search for new types of Christian witnessing communities effective in each of the newly discovered sociological situations. But these sociological "ends of the earth" exist in geographical locations, and witnesses must be sent to them. The base for a world mission is no longer a Western Christendom, but a "Christendom" of churches and disciples diffused all over the globe. Sending can now be from every point on the planet to every point of the compass.

There is many a frontier of strangeness and estrangement to be crossed far or near to a place where a missionary can minister the love of God and proclaim Jesus Christ as Saviour and Lord to unreconciled people who have not known and accepted Him. Bishop Lesslie Newbigin, discussing what activity can be called "missionary" in the context of a world-wide Church, states:

The differentium lies in the crossing of the frontier between faith in Christ as Lord and unbelief. To make clear and to keep clear this, the distinctive meaning of the word "missionary" is one of the most important requirements of the present discussion. He who is sent to make Jesus Christ known and obeyed as Lord among those who do not know and obey Him is a missionary, whether his journey be long or short. The missionary frontier runs through every land where there are communities living without the knowledge of Christ as Lord.[11]

Professor Hoekendijk attacks the idea of the *differentium*, the frontier of unbelief, and of the geographical "end." He says that this concept was employed to define and justify missions alongside other activities of the Church. He holds that it gives spatial categories priority over historical categories and results in no more than "a self-repetition of the Church in an area of unbelief."[12] God forbid! But the historical and sociological categories exist within spatial categories, the Church must emerge from its latent and anonymous state among each and every people, and the command to disciple the nations has to reckon with them as well as with the communities at the place where any church already exists. Near and far the frontier between Church and world is unbelief. Otherwise there would be no distinction between Church and world. The Church exists in the world, of the world, for the world, and yet it is distinct from the world.

Sending is still less a matter of chronology and development of churches than it is of space and distance, achieved when a new church has emerged. It does not end when the sending missionaries under the Holy Spirit have brought new churches into being in geographical "ends of the earth" or Christian cells or other forms of association in any of the new "sociological multiplicities." These new local communities in Christ are themselves required to take up sending as well as evangelism, since each of them is the Church. Much is made of Rufus Anderson's insistence that mission is for planting churches, but it is generally forgotten that he taught that new churches were to engage in sending as well as local proclamation. He declared: "It is impossible for mission churches to reach their highest and truest state, without the aid of that which is to them virtually a foreign mission,—without some outside field of labor for them, resembling the 'hole of the pit' from which they had themselves been digged."[13] The Church is not really the Church unless it sends its bearers of the gospel to the nations. A century after Anderson, Douglas Webster writes:

The surest sign that the gospel has taken root in a new culture is the throwing up of missionaries from that culture to reach out further still. The gospel is received in order to be retransmitted. Missions are integral to genuine Christianity, like all its other scandals.[14]

It must be recognized that today evangelism and sending overlap in effect because of the existence of a global society never before known and instantaneous communication within it. Evangelism is not so locally limited in visibility as it was formerly. The eyes, and especially ears, of peoples in Asia, Africa, and Latin America are fastened upon North America and Europe, South Africa, Australia, and New Zealand, lands predominantly white and nominally Christian. Readers of newspapers and listeners to radio programs in jungle village or mountain town are likely to receive as much news about what is happening in those places as in their own capital cities, perhaps even more. But it is likely to be highly edited, slanted news. There is immediate reporting of killings in race riots and of pray-ins and sit-ins and expulsions from churches in the United States. American national policies and international actions, notably the Vietnam war, are taken to reveal either Christian motivation and principles or the political impotence of Christians. Our very aid programs are taken by some persons to reveal our Christian love for the needy and by others as showing our devotion to self-interest. On the other hand, reports of the involvement of ministers, priests, nuns in struggles for open housing, desegregation of schools, a new deal for the poor, and protest against the war may carry more weight in a decision for Christ in that jungle village or mountain town than a sermon preached on the Beatitudes in the local church.

Moreover, thousands of Americans—the majority nominally Christian—go abroad in the armed services, the diplomatic corps, governmental aid programs, on business, or as tourists. They have opportunity to exercise their evangelistic ministry wherever they may go. Whether they seek to do so or not, their behavior is taken to be illustrative of Christian faith and life. Thousands of persons also come here from other countries, especially as long-term students. Some even come as missionaries of other religions. They observe what religion seems to be in our public life and they report home about it. Therefore, it is indeed true that evangelism has today a world-wide dimension; but that does not eliminate the necessity of the sending of missionaries.

The "nations" and "the ends of the earth" have to be newly discovered in this present day. They are certainly not all geographical. The multitude of sociological entities crying out for the ministry of reconciliation need to be taken seriously and missionaries be sent to them. Sending to those which lie within the borders of the Christian group's own country, America or any other, calls for imaginative, creative thinking and action as well as bold experimentation. But the geographical ends of the earth where there is only a meager or no Christian community, and where the special situations of diverse elements of the population call for multiple forms of witness and ministry, dare not be forgotten because of challenges closer at hand. It is with the messengers and ministering servants of God's people sent into a wide variety of "sociological localities" and distinctive cultural groups within the geographical "ends of the earth" that the following chapters deal. Yet most of what is said probably applies in general to all witnesses to estranged and needy persons and communities within the borders of any Christian's own native land.

Those who are hostile or indifferent to sending missionaries ought to take a lesson from history. It was the sending, limited as it was for many centuries, which kept the Church obedient to its apostolic calling to some degree, and which eventually stimulated local witness and care for lost sheep at home. This is especially evident in the American scene. American home missions arose out of the mission to the Indians and were stimulated to full development by the overseas mission to the distant "heathen." When the missionary societies were founded between 1787 and 1810 they were almost all world-directed, and had as avowed objects, the Indians, the frontier settlements threatened by paganization, and the heathen overseas. But the frontier absorbed all resources and demanded more than the churches would provide until the first missionaries sailed for foreign parts in 1812. The overseas mission imparted the needed stimulus to stewardship and provided the evangelistic impulse which brought forth vision, zeal, men, and money for the apostolic task in the homeland. Home missions could not succeed until foreign missions gave example and inspiration. Then for more than a century it was the overseas mission which continued to cultivate stewardship and to carry forward all denominational causes and nondenominational philanthropic enterprises.

The present recovered vision of "one world mission," the transition from missions to mission, is something for which to thank God. However, the tendency to think that world mission is defined by the American city ghetto and the rural slum, on the one hand, and the lending of personnel and subsidy to needy churches overseas, on the other, is a dangerous misunderstanding of the full apostolate. Excepting when a church is very young and newly come out of paganism into Christ, evangelism has usually flourished only when rooted in and supported by a sending mission. Through many generations it was affirmed that "the light which shines farthest shines brightest at home." If the love of Christ in our hearts is not strong enough to impell us to share it with others beyond the frontiers, it is not powerful enough to make us share it with our neighbors continuously and persistently. Love for home consumption only is not Christian love. Douglas Webster states that the love of God in Jesus Christ is the only motive strong enough to meet the test of theology or of experience, and that "mission is the chariot in which the divine love still comes down in the midst of men." He says further:

The Church, therefore, owes the world its Gospel. It is in debt to Christ and repays that debt only by sharing his love with all mankind. Its missionary task is to find new ways of telling the world about the immeasurable love behind its creation, the deed of love which achieved its salvation, and the triumph of love throughout the universe which is to be the final state and purpose of all things.[15]

The "world" is more than the inner city and the expanding suburbs. Something is strangely awry when in 1967 the oldest world mission board in our nation must cut its program, reduce its budget drastically, and dip deeply into capital funds, not because the churches are failing to give, but because in the name of "our world mission" conferences and associations are taking the lion's share for local work. In the long run it may prove that only "outreach" into all the world can sustain "inreach" into the world at hand.

But there is a factor even more weighty than the lesson of history which should convince us of the necessity of sending. It is the biblical imperative and the insight of the early Church. Local evangelism and service are inherent in the commandment to love neighbor as self because of love of God, but the Great Commission is not primarily addressed to the Christian's neighborhood. Its field is the world. "Go, make disciples of *all nations.*" In the Lukan form in Acts 1:8 Judea and Jerusalem are joined inseparably with Samaria and the ends of the earth. The apostolate is directed to the discipling of the nations— each disciple's own nation and all others. The meaning of nation may now be different than in the time of Christ, but peoples—with their distinctive unity expressed in political and social organization, unique cultures, peculiar world views, religions, needs, loves, hates—form tribes, castes, minorities, subsocieties, and great modern nation states. They are all corporate entities destined to be transformed by the love and power of Christ as well as collections of individuals to whom our Lord is to be introduced personally. In each instance there is a frontier of nonbelief and estrangement to be crossed and a realm of powers in revolt against God to be encountered.

There are many perplexing problems relating to mission, to sending, today. Who are the nations? How is the gospel to be communicated to them? Where are the frontiers? How ought they to be crossed? How do churches within the Church relate to each other in a world mission? What is the relation of the gospel to other faiths? Are there anonymous Christians and a latent Church? If so, how are they to be brought to know their name and to become manifest? But sending cannot be postponed until these questions are answered any more than can local evangelism.

Why send missionaries? Because God has sent the Church to the whole world with the message of salvation. The Church knows that God has given the nations to Christ to be His heritage, and it lives by the hope and conviction "that at the name of Jesus every knee should bow, in heaven and on earth and under the earth, and every tongue confess that Jesus Christ is Lord, to the glory of God the Father" (Phil. 2:10–11).

2

Who Should Go?

The idea of Christian presence is capturing the imagination of a considerable number of youth around the
world, especially through the efforts of the World Student
Christian Federation to foster this concept. It gives sub-
stance to the new emphasis on lay action in ministry
and witness. It makes evangelism come alive to many a
layman. Some members of Asian and African churches
are enthusiastically adopting the idea because they
think that it offers a cheap and easy solution to the thorny
problem of large Western institutions inherited from the
missions and too expensive for the churches to support.
It is supposed that the disciple will live by faith in his
job in secular society and especially in governmental institutions—schools, hospitals, rural extension centers, and
the like—and there so incarnate that faith that it will be
clearly perceived by nonbelievers. He will make his wit-

ness more by life than by voice, but he will speak, too, as he is able.[1] This is indeed the function of every Christian disciple, but the cultivation of Christian presence ought not to prevent adequate wrestling with the difficult questions of the Church's obligations in education, healing, and other forms of service. An important aspect of the concept of presence, and actually a decade older than the current use of the term, is the notion that the era of the lay, "nonprofessional" unsent missionary has arrived. There is a belief abroad that now nobody need be sent because so many are going on their own volition.

"Nonprofessional" Missionaries?

Impressed by the vast multitudes of European and American churchmen living, working, and traveling abroad since the end of World War II, by the visa difficulty of missionaries, and by the hostility of many nationalists in the "Third World" countries toward those professionals, many persons have jumped to the conclusion that individual laymen "on their own" can be unofficial, unpaid, unsent "missionaries." They point to the spontaneous expansion of the Church in the first two centuries through laymen in similar circumstances. If the Church's obligation to carry the faith to the nations can be met in the same manner today, why should anyone go as a professional missionary?

Missionary societies and boards have been trying to give some orientation to laymen going abroad and to alert them to their evangelistic opportunity. This is excellent. However, very few laymen take their evangelistic function so seriously, and the flood of Americans flowing overseas is probably temporary, excepting for tourists. The number of long-term expatriates will probably decrease. The complaints of taxpayers and the adverse balance of payments will gradually decrease the inflated staffs of governmental agencies. It is the policy of new nations to replace foreign employees as fast as nationals can be trained for their posts. Even Western industry and commerce will probably find it politically more advantageous and financially more profitable to be represented in a country by its own nationals. While the boom in overseas travel and service lasts, it is good to try to direct it toward Christian witness as far as possible. Let each disciple of Christ be a nonprofessional evangelist wherever he may be.

There are a few modern counterparts of those early preachers of the gospel and founders of churches. They work in government or secular private schools, medical and health programs, in governmental scientific and technical operations, or in intergovernmental agencies entirely with the aim of discharging a personal missionary vocation. The writer has chanced to meet eight or ten Peace Corps volunteers who regarded their service as Christian mission. A couple teaching in a state university in India at a low salary, uncertain tenure, and no pension prospect is another example. Such persons believe that they can make their Christian witness far more effectively in this manner than if they were employed and sent by churches. They are tent-making missionaries of the order of Saint Paul. May their number increase! This is in truth "Christian presence." Highly skilled professionals in their own fields, they are the true "nonprofessional" missionaries. They must have faith and love in abundance and must account themselves expendable for Christ's sake, because there is no economic security for most of them. But even they will not displace the commissioned and sent missionaries.

Career Missionaries

No matter how many laymen may reside abroad because of their employment or how many may seek overseas employment in order to be a Christian presence, some disciples must always go to represent their brethren whose vocation is to homeland evangelism. Since the Great Commission is to disciple the nations and sending is required to achieve that, then there must be those willing to be sent. As Saint Paul teaches in Romans 12 and Ephesians 4, all members of the body of Christ perform different functions essential to the life and work of the whole and, endowed with various spiritual gifts or ordained to official responsibilities, they are called to work together to exercise the ministry of the Church, that service of reconciliation. Some then must be willing to go so that the full apostolate may be discharged and the nations be brought to Christ.

It is not enough that the gospel be simply announced. It must be communicated with a contagion of faith which will further spread it like wildfire. This can be done only by persons who are themselves on fire with faith. The Church just cannot give the Bible and books on theology or arrange radio and television programs and let it go at that. Because, as potent as these media may be, they lack vital personal testimony to the message. Moreover, the Bible is most effective when preached and taught by a believer.

Ronald Orchard in *Missions in a Time of Testing* points out that any awareness of the Christ-event as the decisive event in history, and even more as the decisive fact for a

man's own personal history, is dependent upon the testimony of persons.[2] He writes:

The clear recognition of and emphasis upon this personal
communication of the Gospel was one of the strengths of foreign missions in the nineteenth century. They were primarily
and distinctively concerned with the sending of persons to proclaim the name of the Redeemer where it was not known. In
doing so they expressed an essential insight into the character
of God's redemptive act, that it was done in a Person—indeed
through *the* Person who is the ultimate standard for our understanding of the meaning of personal existence—and that it
spoke to persons in the center of their being as persons.

Moreover, the missionary has long been the primary
symbol of the supranational and catholic nature of the
Christian faith. Roman Catholics may say that it is the
Pope; but for Protestants and non-Christians alike it
has been the missionary. International, interdenominational, interracial teams or communities might be a better
symbol of the oneness of all peoples reconciled with God
in Christ than is a single missionary in denominational
isolation. Organizations such as the World Council of
Churches may express in a new way the ecumenical unity
of Christians. But in some form and relationship the missionary is the best visible token of the universality of the
gospel. That fact underlies the urgency of having more missionaries today whose color is not white. The missionary is shared love crossing frontiers.

Whenever a nation has turned away from God and
when the Church has failed to call that people to repentance and conversion, God has raised up His prophets to
speak His word. God had to raise up prophets such as
Justinian von Welz and William Carey to call the Protestant churches to missionary obedience. Should the

churches get lukewarm about sending and fail to send missionaries, God will raise them up and send them forth by the Holy Spirit. In fact when today there is so much uncertainty about the sending among denominational churches, the great nondenominational "faith missions" such as the Overseas Missionary Fellowship (former China Inland Mission) and the Latin America Mission, sending forth missionaries out of the churches but apart from them, are prophets of God calling the churches to obedience. For them the trumpet sounds with no uncertain note.

If missionaries must be sent, who should go? A slogan suddenly became popular fifteen years ago when the studies on the "Missionary Obligation of the Church" preparatory to the Willingern Conference were in progress. It was: "Every Christian is a missionary." What this exaggerated declaration really meant was that every disciple by baptism or profession of faith is made a witness to Christ. It would be more correct to say: "Every Christian is meant to be a witness and some must be sent." Is there then a special missionary vocation?

Is There a Missionary Vocation?

The answer throughout the history of Protestant missions has been both No and Yes. Any personal vocation to mission usually comes within the calling of the whole Church to apostolate.[3] There have been many persons who were sure that the Holy Spirit called them specifically to a particular land and people. On the whole, mission directors have been skeptical of such precise, limited vocation. They have been more ready to see the summons of the Spirit in a general call to carry the gospel to the nations, although personal preference might well be expressed and taken into account. In theory, since the whole body of Christ is sent, and in turn sends, to the nations, experienced mission secretaries ought to be able to single out a man or woman for a particular post and say with confidence, "You are the person needed. Go!" That is all the missionary vocation which ought to be required in the Church called to apostolate; and this is the very manner in which most missionaries were called down to the rise of the Roman Catholic missionary orders and congregations and the foundation of Protestant missionary societies. However, those whom we usually call the apostles to various peoples were possessed personally by a passion for mission service. Boniface and Ansgar are examples. Modern mission boards have had special personnel secretaries for almost half a decade, but through most of the first century of American missions there was no recruiting. A candidate was required voluntarily to offer himself. Rufus Anderson, the great mission theorist and administrator of the nineteenth century, advised that only those persons with a strong desire for the work should enter upon it, inspired by an ardent love for the Saviour and a burning zeal for the salvation of men.[4]

Nevertheless, in the opinion of the two greatest American missionary statesmen, Rufus Anderson and Robert E. Speer, that strong desire and decision for service are simply personal recognition of the calling of the whole Church and all its members. They held that because of the nature of the Great Commission and the need of the world, the discipling of the nations takes precedence over local evangelism and pastoral care for each and every disciple. According to that view, it is remaining "at home" that has to be justified. Anderson taught that the Holy Spirit leads the individual to his missionary vocation not by an extraordinary call, but by guiding and illuminating him in a quiet, serious, prayerful study of the gospel, the means of proclamation, one's own abilities and situation, and of God's will for him personally.[5] Speer forcefully restated Anderson's thesis in the pamphlet, "What Constitutes a Missionary Call?"[6] Used by the Student Volunteer Movement, it led thousands upon thousands to dedicate their lives to world mission.

Today, given the post-Christian state of American and European society and the recognition of the difficulty of communicating the gospel to man in our secular culture, it would be difficult—and certainly unconvincing to the missioners in the inner city at least—to argue that distant parts of the earth always have priority. Those who hear the Great Commission personally may think differently, and the Church ought always to be hearing the command to go into both Jerusalem and the end of the earth. Evangelism and sending have equal urgency. Personal qualifications and a conviction about the will of God may lead either way. Since devotion to overseas mission is today very weak in the churches, the call will have to reach many through recruiting secretaries, teachers, pastors, or friends. Many will find this to be the genuine call of the Spirit. The manner of the call is not important, but the call of God and the disciple's answer are important both with respect to the American inner city and the overseas assignment. The conditions of missionary service in many overseas areas, and in some instances in the homeland, are now so characterized by obstacles, misunderstandings, and discouragements that none should enter upon it without a genuine sense of vocation or of doing the will of God as presented in the Church's call. The call of the Holy Spirit, the gift of the

Spirit, and a ministry of the Spirit are all involved in mission now just as in the days of the Apostles.

Motive and Qualifications

No vocation will be answered with complete dedication unless there is strong motivation. Motives to mission have often been mixed. Frequently it has been much the same thing as with a small boy in an Illinois town years ago. His teacher assigned him the writing of an essay on "What I Shall Be When I Grow Up." His paper bore one sentence: "When I grow up I will be a missionary to China, because it is God's work and a fine trip." Throughout the centuries God has been able to use very mixed motives for the advancement of His kingdom if the first of them were love of God and dedication to His will. The Irish missionaries to Europe in the sixth and seventh centuries were largely impelled by ascetic penance, but they wrought great things for God. Bishop Sargent, who has trained many missionaries, says:

The only motive of service that will stand the test of the years is love for the One whose love for us passes all understanding, reaching as it does to the very depths of our being and going out to embrace all men throughout the world. We begin to glimpse something of what that love means when we kneel at Calvary, and it is that glimpse, however obtained, that leads to the prayer, "Lord, here am I. Send me."[7]

A deep love of Christ, issuing in a love of persons and dedication to God's will, can redeem lesser motives and validate the call. Douglas Webster writes: "Stirrings of conscience, an awareness of the deep unmet needs of men, a longing to serve our Lord, a readiness for the unknown, for hardship and for sacrifice, what the old evangelicals called 'a passion for souls,' a real love of people for their own sake as well as for Christ's sake, a deep compassion for human suffering in its many forms—some or all of these may press upon us in such a way that we know we must offer ourselves to go."[8]

Experienced, skillful, sympathetic personnel secretaries of the boards and societies will help a candidate test his motives and his qualifications. If the Church through its proper agency confirms the call by commissioning the candidate after all the rigorous testing and screening which is now the practice, both the missionary and the Church ought to feel assured about the genuineness of vocation and rightness of motivation.

Qualifications are likely to be a test of vocation. The Holy Spirit is not likely to call the actually unqualified. But since self-delusion is possible and human standards of judgment are not those of the Spirit, errors are possible both on the part of the candidate and of his examiners. Bishop Sargent, who reminds us wisely that "Most missionaries are quite ordinary people who have suddenly found themselves called to do something extraordinary," warns also that a mere list of characteristics and qualities desired is terrifying and gives the wrong impression. None is a finished product, and the missionary is in the process of being made by God in the course of service.[9] The missionary is no superman or superwoman.

It is more than interesting—it is illuminating—to see what the qualifications of missionaries have been said to be through the past two and a half centuries. The eighteenth-century list put first the missionary's relationship to our Lord.[10] He was expected to be "a man of God" (all missionaries were then men) who knows Jesus Christ personally by head and heart. An experiential knowledge of the working of the Holy Spirit within him was deemed essential. There should have been personal overcoming of temptation. The missionary was expected to be one in whose life Christ is revealed. Such a person requires wisdom, courage, patience, self-denial, prudence, humility, "mortification to this world," and zeal for the honor of God. Ability to learn a vernacular language was rated high. Superior intellectual attainment is to be matched by moral qualities: renunciation of comforts and familiar ways and friends, extraordinary devotion to duty, singleness of purpose, love for the souls of men and benevolence toward human need, ignorance, and weakness. Genuine piety was always listed. The man who in the next century supervised and counseled more missionaries than any other individual and who never sentimentalized them, Rufus Anderson, said that the missionary needed no general qualifications other than those required of all ministers. The missionary's circumstances demanded more patience, perseverance, and self-denial, but the only special qualities in Anderson's view are more than usual ardent love for Christ, burning zeal for the salvation of men, and a powerful desire to do the work.[11]

What are the qualifications which the experts want today? Douglas Webster's statement quoted above reiterates the same basic qualities as those stressed one and two hundred years earlier. He further describes the desired characteristics as being a personal knowledge of Jesus Christ, a capacity to interpret the gospel, an awareness of the kind of world in which we live, and a readiness to make the universal Church a reality.[12] Anderson would have agreed with Webster, although his understanding of the Church would have been somewhat different. Awareness of a revolutionary world is the one big change, but Anderson also wanted the missionary to know the world of his day.

The qualities desired in a missionary by Bishop Sargent, who has trained many missionaries and observed them in service, are found in his chapter headings.[13] After love of Christ the next most important quality is friendship for people, genuine friendliness that can express itself in ways congenial to the people among whom he lives and seeks fellowship. Sargent's desired qualities are to be deduced from the nouns which he uses to describe the varying roles of the missionary: the friend, the learner, the evangelist, the colleague, the servant, the help (i.e., RSV "helper," 1 Cor. 12:28), and finally the saint. A saint is one set apart for God's service and one "truly Christ-like in all the daily intercourse of life."[14] He recalls that Bishop Stephen Neill puts sainthood first among all the qualities to be looked for in the modern missionary.[15] Sainthood is not the old pietistic otherworldly stereotype.

Bishop Ralph E. Dodge, having the African scene especially in view, names nine qualifications of the missionary.[16] First of all, the missionary must be free from self and dedicated to the will of God. Then follow flexibility, a winsome personality, complete sincerity, the will and ability to share in warm friendship, humility and a readiness to learn, thorough grounding in faith, and a keen sensitivity to the feelings of others. The bishop also wants the man or woman to be secure in the home environment from which he goes out, and in the new environment into which he enters he calls for ability to work effectively on a basis of equality with nationals in a changing, competitive society.

John Carden, in *The Ugly Missionary*, makes no lists, but one ends the tour of missions with him concluding that the major qualities needed today are love, commitment, and acceptance of servanthood. James A. Scherer's statement of "qualities of a great missionary" include: apostolic mentality, i.e., a clear consciousness of what God requires and zeal for the gospel arising from the will of God, superb mental equipment, a gift for communicating the Christian faith and for sharing the Christian life, life commitment, spiritual depth, and costly identification.[17] The Korean churchman Dr. Ji Won Yong writes: "When a national pastor or evangelist can meet the missionary face to face with no emotional barriers, as a person and a colleague, mission endeavor, humanly speaking, will prosper. It is necessary for the missionary today to have more personality than intelligence, more sincerity than knowledge, more humility than precept. Nothing can replace the new posture of genuine humility with grace and good will. It is also necessary that he be more Christian than the businessman-type mission executive, more "pastor" than "missionary," more friend than an American or strong representative of a foreign "ecclesiology."[18] Jacob A. Loewen, a sensitive, discerning, courageous missionary, puts "role sincerity" high as a requirement—the ability consistently to carry out to the very end the role which the missionary has consciously assumed among a people.[19]

Here, on the whole, are the same old missionary virtues on which all have agreed, headed by love of God and man and dedication to both. The three new notes sounded strongly in recent times emerge clearly in this review. They are humble servanthood, flexibility and initiative amid revolutionary change, and identification.

Servanthood is indeed a prime requirement now. He who wants to be a boss and lord it over nationals had better not go. Despite all that was said about love and sacrifice and service, the missionary in the old era was in-

deed a lord in the churches and a power in the land,
a person identified with the might of a colonial regime
or considered identified with foreign power. The greatest
shock to China missionaries after expulsion was not their
rejection by the Communist regime, but our belated discovery that Chinese colleagues so bitterly resented our
often unconscious attitude of superiority and means of
indirect control. Dr. Ji Won Yong says that a superiority
complex is the worst enemy of the missionary. The humility required today is the inescapable price to be paid for
effective service, and it is useful service in national
churches and among people outside them that finds a
welcome. Did not our Lord wash the feet of His disciples
and tell them: "I have given you an example, that you
also should do as I have done to you" (John 13:15)? In
addition to servanthood, circumstances require that the
Western missionary humbly bear the sins of the West
toward much of the rest of the world. Philip Potter,
executive of the Division of World Mission and Evangelism of the World Council of Churches, recalling the
former arrogance of missionaries in looking down and
talking down from the heights of power, prestige, and self-
righteousness, says that at last today the American missionary has lost his "innocence" and must walk as a humble
sinner among sinners. He cannot now go to others without
consciousness of American action in Vietnam and race
riots in American cities.

Flexibility and initiative cannot be minimized. There
is more change in a decade now than there used to be in a
century. A missionary cannot expect a job description
that will remain constant to the end of his career. What a
contrast between the minutely detailed instructions
which directors of the societies handed to early Protestant missionaries and the stable patterns which persisted

for a century and the present call for flexibility! Now in a time of rapid and radical social, economic, political, and ecclesiastical change flexibility, imagination, and initiative are indispensable qualities even in an institutional assignment under a national church.

Identification is only love matured—thoroughgoing love which makes a foreigner one with the people among whom he lives despite his origin and the alien culture that clings to him. Even in the old days of the lordly missionary there were plenty of instances of identification even though the man or woman might appear to be a foreign body in the community. For example, when agitators demanded that the people of Sungkiang kill or drive out the "foreigner," they exclaimed in astonishment, "That is no foreigner! That is Pastor Burke, an old Sungkiang man!" Fifteen years ago mission leaders were vigorously stressing identification through cultural appreciation and conformity, simpler living, and the like. Then for a decade or more little was heard about it, and the missionary was told to stay American, English, or German.

Now identification at a deeper level is being required. When the Archbishop of East Africa (Anglican) was asked what kind of missionaries are wanted, he replied: "The Church would wish to call its own missionaries rather than just have them placed in its territory. The message for those who choose to throw in their lot with this self-governing Church would be: 'Leave us your bones.' They would be missionaries who would desire to be intimately associated for the rest of their lives with the people of East Africa."[20] This is a picturesque way of saying that such persons should be prepared to invest a lifetime in growth in unity with the people, becoming one with them by proficiency in language, sensitivity to social values, warmth in friendship, and gladness in the fellowship of service. Jacob A. Loewen points out that when a newcomer enters a highly structured primitive society, its members will not know how to act toward him until he has been incorporated into this network of relationships. Identification will then depend upon the role which he assumes or which the people give to him.[21] Loewen bears impressive testimony to the need of reciprocity in identification.[22] This involves a willingness not only to learn and know, but to be known, requiring a readiness to sacrifice privacy. He writes: "In the missionary-national relationship, if ours is a genuine concern to know and to be known and to develop a genuine reciprocal relationship, we must remember that no amount of externality will be sufficient. While we may overtly express real interest, if this is not the genuine attitude of our heart, we will be in serious difficulty." And this must be on a personal and individual level. Reciprocity involves further a bidirectional flow of communication. It involves accepting and respecting a people's approach to reality and society as equally valid with one's own. But in the end any cultural appreciation and adaptation take second place to love and friendship and mutual appreciation. A Korean friend of mine commented sadly about an American who made much of "equality" and friendship but who each time they met called him by a different surname!

Present circumstances are such that there is little security for the missionary, and he must count himself expendable. He may be eliminated by some government's decree or by the will of some church. One great American mission agency has recently decided not to make appointments for life but for terms only. Yet if there is not life commitment in a quest for identification through diligent learning, making of friendships, and servant ministry there will be little growth in grace or fruitful service.

There is redundancy in that phrase "servant ministry" because ministry means servanthood.

The swift pace of revolutionary change and need for identification commit to continuous and unceasing learning the man or woman who is sent and goes. That he should already have had a sound education in Christian faith is self-evident, but in a strange situation he is required to study that faith anew from unfamiliar perspectives. Cultural values and religious insights different from those at home pose quite different questions, and answers acceptable in the West may be unacceptable elsewhere. Consequently, there should be a deeper delving into Bible and theology and a more profound attempt to relate gospel to culture. If before leaving home the new missionary has some introduction to linguistics, to a particular language, and to the land and its culture, he is fortunate. But this will have been only at the "nursery school" level of learning. Intimate, appreciative understanding of another language and culture are among the priceless rewards of missionary service. It is gained only at the cost of endless observation, study, and identification. Now, too, the books one reads are out-of-date before they are published, and knowledge of the cultural heritage must be related to present rapid change.

Moreover, this changing local situation has to be related to a changing world situation, also to the state of affairs "back home," and even in the churches there. A missionary who is not alert can get out of touch with all reality everywhere and live in a world that has vanished. Add to all this the necessity of keeping up with professional literature and techniques, if one is a specialist, and the commitment to learning assumes colossal proportions. Insatiable curiosity and a thirst for knowledge are good qualities in a missionary. It should not be a matter for surprise that so many men and women forced to return home have taken up so wide a variety of jobs and services. Any keen missionary has been a student in the most remarkable of schools.

Finally, it should be noted that the contemporary missionary faces greater uncertainty and insecurity than most of his spiritual forefathers. Some missionaries were martyred, others faced hostility and persecution, far more died of disease (think of the terrific death toll in the Wesleyan and Basel missions on the Gold Coast!), more were invalided home, and there were hardships in pioneering.[23] Yet the alliance of missions with colonial power and the all-conquering European culture, or at least the trappings of its civilization, gave the missionary prestige, influence, and physical security. Gradually the physical conditions of life became exceedingly easy and comfortable. A board or society was behind its representative abroad, although financial support was always a matter of faith. The missionary could confidently expect a lifetime of service.

Now that security has vanished. This is hard for security-conscious Americans. Oh, there is still marvelous economic security, although certainly not wealth, under a paternalistic system of allowances so long as the person serves his board, but tenure is now exceedingly uncertain. A government may refuse a residence permit to someone returning from furlough, or it may expel all missionaries. Nationalistic antiforeignism may make life uncomfortable. The missionary may come to feel that the national church with which he is associated may not want him or does not know how to use him. Civil war, internal commotions, and invasions may create physical dangers. No, there is now nothing certain about job tenure and financial security, nor in some places about safety for family and self. A generation ago it seemed most ludicrous to talk about the missionary taking up his cross and following Christ in danger, hardship, and suffering. It was downright embarrassing when people talked to us about our nonexistent hardships and sacrifices. The old pietist hero worship and glorification of the missionary died hard. Now there is more relevance in the idea. At least it is an ever-present possibility that there may be some suffering and even more an interruption of ministry.

Every generation of mission preachers has reminded the missionary that he has the promise of the Divine Presence, the very companionship of our Lord, and the gift of the Holy Spirit for power in his work. He who would go to the nations ought to practice that Presence, and, if he does, he will have in his heart the peace that passes all understanding. It is not the peace of self-confidence or of assurance of exemption from hardship and danger, but rather the serenity of faith and trust. This fruit of the Lord's companionship and knowledge that God's power can make up the deficiency of human weakness rescue the disciple from fear and panic. With such peace in his heart, the one who has been sent can bear trials, hardship, and danger. He can see his career suddenly end and long years of effort and preparation appear to come to nothing, but then turn with confidence and determination to a new post of witness and perhaps even cross a new frontier. Him who goes we may well dispatch with the ancient Chinese commendation: "I lu p'ing-an"—"Peace be with you all the way."

3

How Do Others See the Missionary?

It is usually a shocking experience when for the first time a person hears his recorded voice or sees and hears himself on closed-circuit television. But this makes possible corrections of faults and improvement in speaking. Similarly it may be painful, but it is salutary for the modern missionary to see himself as others see him.

The missionary has always been seen out of focus or in distortion by many persons, both friends and foes. Novelists, caricaturists, and cartoonists have ridiculed him, maligned him, misrepresented him, and "poked fun" at him. His friends in the churches, on the contrary, have all too often regarded him as a spiritual superman or superwoman, have romanticized him, glorified him, and dehumanized him in the process. It is rare when a novelist has dealt honestly with the missionary. James Michener has done so in *Hawaii*, despite the outcries of critics in re-

ligious circles. He has understood the pioneers of the
Sandwich Islands Mission—their fallible humanity, their
being creatures of New England Puritan society, their
consequent cultural blindness and unconscious arrogance,
but he has also understood their genuine faith and passion
for souls.

Novelists and writers of travelogues have frequently
represented the missionary as a religious bigot, intolerant of other faiths and even of Christian denominations
other than his own, a rank proselytizer. There has in the
mission through the ages been much intolerance of other
religions, because this has been a major force in Christian tradition. Yet there also has been from the first days
of the Church another attitude which finds truth of
God's giving in all religions as well as in nature as the
work of Christ, the creative pre-existent *Logos*. Missionaries have been among the best and most sympathetic
interpreters of Asian and primitive religions and trans-
lators of their scriptures. Some denominational rivalry
among Christians has unhappily been transported overseas, but ecclesiastical imperialism and rivalry were late-
comers to world mission, and Protestant missionaries felt
and practiced unity to a degree seldom known in their
homelands until recently. Look at the system of comity
which developed![1] By a division of territory they sought
to eliminate waste of effort through overlapping and to
keep differences in worship and teaching from causing confusion in the minds of people. Remember that the contemporary Ecumenical Movement is the child of the
overseas mission.

Anthropologists have damned the missionary for destroying primitive cultures. But scarcely any nineteenth-
century European or American had any regard and esteem
for any civilization other than his own. "Culture" or

"civilization" could only be European. The mission has been a powerful force for cultural change, yet it was only one of many factors which exerted a disintegrating impact on primitive societies. Colonial governments, commerce, exploitation of the land and minerals, introduction of new diseases, more potent forms of alcohol, and forced labor were even more powerful. The Christian religion was often the one positive force directing the change, and the missionaries were constantly the protectors and champions of the people before government and against exploiting agencies.

Nevertheless, the cartoonist liked to portray the austere, emaciated, disapproving foreigner destroying simple folk pleasures and spreading gloom or boiling in the pot of some cannibal. Today the missionary is indeed in the pot, stewing in his own uncertainties and frustrations, or being roasted by the fiery attacks of nationalists, members of young churches, and even his fellows in the churches at home who supposedly have sent him.

At Home Base

The missionary is an anachronism in the sight of a large part of the American populace at present. He is considered a vestige of a remote time when we believed ourselves superior to other peoples and reached down a hand from on high to lift them up. Even in the churches all is not well with the mission enterprise. American churchmen are giving more money to missions than ever before, but impersonally, without commitment and participation. Many doubt the rightness of it. It is a scandal to present Jesus Christ as the only Saviour and the supreme revelation of God to other people who have their own religion and modes of salvation. Christ as sole Saviour has been in every generation a scandal to men of other faiths and no faiths when first so presented to them, but it is a new thing that He should be a scandal to those who bear His name. How many mothers today dedicate an unborn child to God's service in mission? Now it is thought good to alleviate suffering and to help peoples to attain modernity and a larger share in the physical goods of life, but it is deemed wrong to "meddle" with their religion or indigenous system of values. Therefore, Americans are willing that our impersonal government spend billions of dollars on aid programs and loans for development and send forth Peace Corps volunteers. The Church's acceptable counterpart activity may be the sending of some ecclesiastical, eduational, medical, and social service experts to assist young sister churches and the granting of some money to subsidize them. So it happens that the missionary who is the symbol of God's calling of all people to Him and of the Church's part in that calling makes many of his fellow Christians uncomfortable, and they stay away from church when he or she comes to speak about the work.

There is great hostility on the campuses to mission, and while only a small minority are personally interested and committed a vast number avidly seek information about the Oriental religions. The Peace Corps, the Papal Volunteers, British Overseas Service, and such agencies are considered better means of helping other peoples and of discharging the individual's responsibility for service to mankind. Moreover, since such volunteer workers receive only subsistence allowances and live and work at grassroots relationships with people, students tend to regard as "phony" the missionary who pretends to servanthood, but lives in a large bungalow apart from the people, relying on refrigerators and American gadgets, driving a car while his national colleague rides a bicycle or walks. A Peace Corps volunteer in training said: "Everything we read and hear from lecturers in the course of our study makes it appear that the missionaries did everything wrong. Granted that they made mistakes and did much that was wrong, it just cannot all have been bad. Give me some references to books and records which will show the truth." All that the missionary can ask from critical youth is an effort to understand what he really wants to do and an objective appraisal of what he has done.

Critics Within the Young Churches

The most damning and bitter charges leveled at the missionary come from persons whose esteem, good will, and love he should most desire. These are fellow ministers and members in those churches which have grown as the fruits of the mission. Too many Christian nationals say that the missionary keeps aloof from them; that he is walled off from them by pride, a sense of superiority, and his self-importance, by a clannishness that limits his social contacts to other missionaries. They say, too, that he exerts unfair control through the purse strings long after official control has been formally surrendered. They charge that he keeps the national church in a confessional or denominational strait jacket. It is said that basically the missionary as a species lacks love. Just because he is a missionary—and usually a white man—he thinks that he knows everything and is the final authority on every subject.

This writer has heard this theme with every possible variation during every visit into Africa and Asia. Foreign students in America repeat it. Scarcely a week goes by that it is not reiterated in some document or piece of literature. A recent instance to come to my attention is a confidential report of a discussion of church-mission relationships by a small group of Indians and missionaries related to one church in southern India. The nationals were unusually outspoken. It is reported that the Indians think the chief handicap in the relationship to be the missionaries' maddening sense of superiority and their aloofness. There is also a lack of real identity and genuine friendship. An Indian feels that he is not free to go into a missionary's home. Should he go and happen to find the family at a meal, the Indian will wait; but if a missionary comes at that time he will go right on in and be asked to share the meal. A request for a conversation is likely to be treated as a petition for an interview with a V.I.P. and must be justified by having to do with a matter of great importance in the eyes of the foreigner. It was said that missionaries actually show little interest in the work of the church unless they direct it or are deeply involved personally in it. Real international friendships are rare even among ministers, according to this report.

It may be a matter of surprise to critics, but actually there is no other large-scale long-continuing enterprise which has a better record of self-criticism than Protestant overseas missions. Beginning with the Edinburgh Conference of 1910, such cooperative self-analysis has been undertaken periodically through study and discussion in connection with a series of world conferences. Earlier conferences were descriptive and promotional. Since 1910 the world conferences, national ones, and studies made by denominational boards have critically studied and pondered almost every aspect of world mission and its implementation. Individual scholars add their contributions. The older literature on the missionary had more to do with his recruitment and training. Now many scholars have been analyzing the missionary in his present predicament. They have been very frank in reporting their findings. It is needful for us to listen to what some of the most trusted educators and supervisors of missionaries have to say.

Bishop Sargent reports a Chinese student as saying: "I am actually very disappointed with the results of the new treaties. We had always thought that the attitude of superiority adopted by Westerners was due to the unequal treaties. Under the new agreements we looked for a change. But you are still the same. We have to try to realize now that a feeling of superiority is part of your make-up." The Bishop continues: "A national pride which leads to the despising of other men, consciously or unconsciously, is as damnable as the more personal variety. It is often the dominant element in the first impression which we give people of other races."[2] With the soul-searching post-mortem investigation of the China situation after 1950 we all thought that this was one of the most important lessons which we had learned, but a decade and a half later this same charge of pride is being heard again and again.

Bishop Ralph E. Dodge writes about the present "wave of antagonism" to Christianity in Africa, and reports that this severe criticism of the Church "comes from *within*—it comes from second generation Christians, and it comes with a force and bitterness that is convincing."[3] He presents the facts behind his title, *The Unpopular Missionary*. The criticisms made by African youth he takes to be in the interest of the Church and regards them as much more moderate than those made by persons outside the Christian community. The charges run: The missionaries were the forerunners of imperialism and still today remain as the agents of a lingering colonialism. They are part and parcel of the dominant and domineering white ruling element. They failed to give Africans opportunity for leadership in the Church and refused to train them for responsibility in either Church or state. Even in the new independent nations the missionary still rules the churches and represses his African colleagues. He still considers Africans inferior and segregates them, even burying his dead in segregated cemeteries apart from Africans.

The Church is the white man's Church, according to the critics whom the Bishop has heard. He quotes a secondary school lad as saying: "We are going to do away with the established churches in this country and then we shall build our own church based on the teachings of Christ." There is bitterness over bosses trying to perpetuate power, lacking in love, being moved at the best by pity. Pity was for centuries a strong missionary motive, and in this connection it is good to note a word by the Korean Dr. Ji Won Yong that empathy is greater than sympathy and requires a higher price. Pity excludes identification, and it is resented. Bishop Dodge states that the seven most serious charges are: inability to communicate (including failure to learn the language), unsympathetic attitude, lack of understanding, inability to produce results, failure to identify, lack of cooperation, and a desire for segregation. The foreigners are said to preach a limited gospel, to separate religion from the rest of life, just as they segregate themselves from Africans socially, whereas African religion permeates and integrates the whole life of men. The missionary, it is claimed, still despises African culture and keeps it out of the churches. He fosters a purely European tradition of worship and devotional life. Disunity is perpetuated by the missionaries for the sake of their jobs, and this is a scandal.

Such statements add up to a serious indictment, but the worst charge is hypocrisy. One student complained: "The weakness of the church is due to the fact that the missionaries preach in church, telling people to love their neighbors but they themselves do not love their neighbors. The missionary school man is good only when he is at school. If you meet him in town, he shows you his true colours and does not recognize you." The emotional outbursts of students seem to the writer to become even more violent when they come to America to study, if the diatribes voiced by African students at the University of Chicago over the past ten years afford a fair sample of opinion and may be taken as typical. What is most disquieting is the fact that the vehement statements of the students are all too often supported by the reports of scholars. One of the mildest of such judgments is this word of E. A. Asamosa:

European missionaries should, in the first place, acknowledge that there is a section of the African "mind" which they have not yet been able to penetrate—or rather, that there is a sphere of the African soul-world which they have not yet been able to enter. To be able to do so would mean coming out of the citadels of their own religious heritage and prejudices and taking a venture into wide, unexplored fields of knowledge.[4]

The last sentence might be italicized.

As one talks with African Christians in the United States and in their homes, he is impressed by the constant reiteration of resentment against pride, superiority, lack of love, and, above all, the closing of the missionary home to African colleagues and fellow Christians. Free sharing of the home seems not just in Africa but everywhere to be taken as genuine proof of the absence of pride

and superiority, of true love and friendship, of actual identification. Many Africans speak bitterly of being required
always to go to the missionary's back door. One distinguished church leader related how tea was served to the
African and white members of the staff of a certain institution in two different places at the same hour. Eventually the Africans were invited to join the white staff on
the same veranda. But tea was served to the two groups
out of separate teapots and with different sets of china!
The cleavage was all the more apparent. Admission to a
home is not enough. There must be a real sharing. Loewen tells about a North American woman among Central American Indians who found it extremely difficult to
allow Indians to come into her house. She made a special
effort therefore to invite Christians there for coffee on
Sunday afternoons. Later some of them said to Loewen:
"You know, we have never been able to enter that
woman's home." He remonstrated, reminding them of the
Sunday afternoon visits. The national responded: "Yes,
we've been in her house, but she has never opened her
home to us. That is closed for all nationals."[5] On another
occasion a group of Indians were talking about a deceased
missionary, and remarked that she had felt that they were
dirty. She always wiped off the chairs and floor as soon as
they left. And that was supposed to be a secret among the
missionaries only! As Dr. Ji says, "The Creator gave the
common people a good trait to be sensitive to the human
situation; they know very well whether the missionary is
really interested in them or just tries to use them."

The language may be somewhat different, the complaints may take slightly different forms, but one hears
much the same thing in country after country and from
critical, but sympathetic, observers who are themselves
part of the missionary enterprise. James A. Scherer, Dean

of the Lutheran School of Missions, says that many Christians are shouting, "Missionary, go home!" because of the strategic, diplomatic, and spiritual failure of the missionaries.[6] He states that the lack of men with apostolic gifts has left the mission "bogged down in trench warfare." Having outlived his role as pioneer and supervisor, the average missionary has not yet found his new role of servant and friend. He has spent himself in good works but "has not succeeded in imbuing the church with a zest for being in God's work or for loving its neighbors." That is what troubles one most, the lack of evangelistic zeal on the part of many younger churches. Is it because the missionary's love has not been strong enough to be the conduit of the love of Christ, which when once passed on to people cannot be retained by them but must be given by them to others still?

John Carden quotes the Home Secretary of the Church Missionary Society as saying: "There is no doubt that today the word *missionary* is a very dirty word."[7] The remainder of his statement is: "But viewed in its proper context, has it ever been anything else . . . ? And if it be really true of us that we are regarded as outcasts, commonplace, not very well educated, sometimes despised, jolted around, and even mocked, ought we not rather to rejoice at this because at last we might be beginning to get near to our true vocation?"

If it were only just persons of other faiths who were mocking us, we might take comfort in remembering our Lord's words: "Blessed are you when men revile you and persecute you and utter all kinds of evil against you falsely on my account" (Matt. 5:11). But it is impossible to convince ourselves that the reviling of us is really on Christ's account when the allegations come from our own brethren in the faith. It is more to the point to remember that we members in the body of Christ are expected to heed the admonitions and reproof of our brethren, and that our Lord instructed us: "This is my commandment, that you love one another, as I have loved you" (John 15:12).

The Critics in Other Religions

The most bitter despising and mocking comes from outside the churches. It is in large measure one form of nationalistic antiforeignism and anti-imperialism rampant in the new nations and in the remaining colonial areas. It is also an act of aggressive retaliation which can be freely voiced by adherents of other religions as they remember what seems to them unfair Christian aggression in the past. It has been stimulated by the Chinese Communists' indictment of the "crimes" of the missionaries, on the one hand, and, on the other, by scholarly studies by Asians and Africans, such as K. M. Panikkar's *Asia and Western Dominance*. It is a continuing protest against the long alliance of the mission with European political, military, and economic power and with the once-conquering European civilization. Concessions enacted in the "unequal treaties," the protection afforded by gunboats and marines, and the exacting of indemnities for deaths and property damage are memories still very much alive. But there is something much more immediate and personal also in most complaints.

The writer of this book has made an effort during travels in the last decade and more to learn what the followers of other religions think about Christianity. The result has been to a large degree to discover what they think about the missionary. He is to them the most conspicuous representative of Christianity, and they believe that as its official propagator he must really incarnate his faith. They also suppose that it is still the missionary who dictates to national Christians what they must believe and how they should act. He is thought "to hold them in line."

There is in Asia, especially along its eastern rim, a lively interest in Christianity, much like the fascination which the Oriental religions exert upon American students and intellectuals. Part of it is due to the general revival of religions and to concern for all things religious, while part of it is a desire to know the enemy in order to attack him. It is partly also a search for forms, methods, and programs to be borrowed and adapted to the use of Asian religions. The adherent of any religion who is ready to listen to and to learn from others has plenty of opportunity to answer questions about his own faith, but any Christian wanting a hearing must be ready first to hear patiently and then to deal honestly with complaints. These charges arrange themselves into about eight major objections and criticisms.

Always first is the denunciation of Christianity's intolerance. The Asian religions, excepting Islam, have long since ceased aggression toward one another. They have lived in mutual toleration, and have borrowed from each other. Singhalese Buddhism's discrimination toward people of other faiths in Ceylon is a rare exception. In most instances I countered this charge with the assertion that the Christian population in the country was far too small to deny religious liberty to others or to subject them to discrimination. Was it not rather the exclusiveness of Christianity, its claim to the total allegiance of the disciple, and its abhorrence of syncretism to which objection was really being voiced? Yes, comes the answer, and such exclusiveness is arrogant. But in addition, they say, there is a deep-rooted spirit of intolerance, and it is manifested in the attitude and behavior of missionaries. Alas! Too many unhappy examples could be given.

A high Buddhist dignitary related how on the holiest day of the religious year at the celebrated Temple of the Tooth in Kandy, Ceylon, a party of American missionaries put up a tent opposite the main entrance to the temple and, using an amplifier, all day long attacked the personal character of the Buddha and denounced his teaching. Similarly it was related in Japan that missionaries of a certain society, whenever there has been a conversion, hold a ceremony on the street before the house and burn the Buddhist home altar or Shinto god-shelf to the accompaniment of belittling of the impotent gods and loud rejoicing. In the Middle East it will be remembered for generations that a certain missionary climbed the minaret of a mosque and shouted from its top that there is no God but God and Jesus Christ is His only begotten Son. The list of atrocities is long and disheartening, all contrary to the spirit of our Lord and all hindrances to true and effective evangelism. But it is widely believed that this is the missionary spirit.

Another complaint closely related to the first is that Christians are also exclusive in another sense. They hold themselves to be superior to all others and live apart, disassociating themselves from their fellow citizens and refusing to participate in the community life. There are places where the Christians admit to separateness and defend it on the grounds of minority status, the need for solidarity and self-preservation, and of guarding against contamination by paganism. Ghetto life, either physically or psychologically, effectively cuts off all opportunity for Christian witness and leads to an ingrown and atrophied community. The critics blame this kind of exclusiveness and separatism on the missionaries. They say that it has rubbed off the missionaries onto the Christians—the very same pride and lovelessness. The national Christians catch it from their foreign mentors by contagion and the latter actually imbue them with it. A distinguished Hindu university professor told about a national conference of representatives of religions devoted to the subject of "saints." The Christians had been warmly invited, but only one Roman Catholic priest attended. He added sadly, "The Christians would not even share their saints with us." But fortunately there are outstanding examples of the opposite sort. This writer was taken to the holy city of Hardwar on the Ganges, where he had once been chased away as a foreigner and devotee of another religion, by an American Presbyterian minister and a French Roman Catholic Benedictine priest who live the life and wear the garb of the Indian holy man. The swamis and sanyasin joyfully received them as brothers and courteously received their friend for their sakes. Those missionaries have no difficulty in speaking about the gospel and getting a hearing. Such persons give the lie to the frequently made assertion that Christians still have to join the human race.

One hears, further, that missionaries teach Christians to judge others, including members of other churches of the same faith, not by fundamentals of doctrine, ethics, and character, but by petty moralism. Christian missionaries are said to be archfoes of simple pleasures and the propagators of a kill-joy religion of gloom and negation. Petty prohibitions are demanded by the missionaries and perpetuated by the national pastors, their apt pupils. Mere social customs and preferences are confused with principles of religion. Participation in folk festivals, drinking a cup of sake, smoking a cheroot, joining in a staff party of the employing company—all these pleasures are forbidden. These seem to missionaries to be far more important than doctrine or ethics. Such requirements of church membership reflect, indeed, the social prejudices and pietistic outlook of many of the founding missionaries, but they are now demanded by the inertia of tradition more often than by the insistence of missionaries. They are matters for churches to determine now, but missionaries can encourage nationals to study afresh on the basis of Bible, theology, and stewardship what are the real marks of Christian life and requirements of church membership. It was not foreign imposition but spontaneous indigenous consensus of the most practical sort which led a church of Indians in Panama, all recently rescued from the degradation of drunkenness, to require total abstinence of themselves and, having no wine, to use sweet sugarcane juice instead of the local potent liquor in the Lord's Supper.

Two closely related complaints heard in Asia, if not in Africa, are the neglect of spiritual discipline and meditation and the ugliness of the Christian cultus. It is said that the missionaries have introduced mere activism in place of religion and that they do not know how quietly to wait on God for illumination. The Western faith therefore, they claim, cannot meet the deepest hungers of the Eastern mind and heart. One finds some converts now leaving Christianity and returning to Buddhism on this account, as happened in considerable numbers in China about thirty years ago during the revival led by the monk T'ai Hsü. A Zen master in Japan said to the writer that if Western Christians want to converse and discuss with Buddhists, the beginning should be made in meditation with them. Asian people have heard little or nothing about Christian mysticism from missionaries, and have had to discover it themselves. Only about half a dozen missionaries are living the integrated and well-balanced contemplative-active life in the Indian Christian ashrams.

Missionaries from churches which confuse the spiritual with the mental and the "world" or the flesh with the emotions have tended to create austere and barren places and forms of worship in the young churches. Those who come from denominations which reacted violently against Roman Catholic, Orthodox, and Protestant state churches were likely to outlaw beauty and color from buildings, liturgy, and devotional practice. Even major denominations which have done better in their homelands are sad offenders in this matter. Religion provided most of the color and joy in the drab life of the masses for centuries. Conversion to Christian faith ought not to rob them of beauty, variety, and drama. This is a matter, however, in which the critics are for the most part really blaming the contemporary missionary for the sins of the fathers rather than for his own.

The criticism made with most force and heat is that Christianity is utterly foreign and that the missionary is not only the primary symbol of its alien nature but also a foreign agent subversive of national welfare. Memories are long, and the old association of missions with imperialism and nationalism has not been forgotten. Even Great Britain's vaunted colonial policy of religious neutrality and nonintervention is now regarded as having been discriminatory in favor of Christianity. But the baffling fact is that thousands of persons actually believe that missions today are used and subsidized by Western governments for political purposes. Perhaps this is because ecclesiastical colonialism lingers on so long after political colonialism has ended.

Foreign money in the hands of foreign agents strikes fear into the minds of many nationals. This was one of the chief causes behind the notorious and unobjective report on missionary activities made by a committee of the Indian state of Madhya Pradesh in 1956.[8] This fear along with other factors leads to visa restrictions, residence limitations, and expulsion of missionaries from aboriginal areas or from the whole country. Even in tolerant Thailand one hears it argued that missionaries ought to be kept away from mountain tribes. It is not hard to understand how such views about the relations of missionaries to government can arise in a colony such as Hong Kong where special favors and aid are granted to churches and missions. But how can persons in Japan believe that missionaries, Christian institutions, and even Japanese pastors and local congregations are supported by foreign government funds? Many have said to the writer that they have no objection to thousands of their fellow citizens and co-religionists becoming Christians through their own private spiritual pilgrimage but that they resent their being bought by foreign agents with foreign money. Many Buddhists have said: "If our government would support our missions like your government subsidizes yours, there would be as many Japanese missionaries in America as there are Americans here." Such misunderstandings are a grave handicap to the local Christians and to the missionary, both of whom must live down the old associations with imperialism and colonialism. The urgency for identification becomes all the greater when such suspicions are current.

Even when persons adhering to other religions do not regard the missionary as a foreign political agent, they may still fear that he is dangerous to the political welfare of the country because they believe that Christianity itself is by nature politically and socially divisive. Disunity among Christians is regarded as a scandal in itself and this works against acceptance of the message of reconciliation. Again and again one hears that Christians preach brotherhood, unity, and equality, but that dominant whites practice segregation and repression against church members of other races. Islam, it is said, achieves the brotherhood which Christianity merely claims to have. Christianity preaches peace, but actually it foments war, imperialism, colonial exploitation, and world turmoil, according to many followers of Gautama, whereas Buddhism actually provides a spiritual basis for national and world-wide peace and a just social order.[9]

Each and every new nation today needs unity and stability, and it is the present internecine strife among Christians that is the chief source of worry. Throughout two and a half centuries missionaries from all nations and all denominations, with few exceptions, formed one family and fellowship. Unhappily, now discord is exported and fostered from America and other Western quarters. Rival associations are created and charges are hurled against the older churches and their agencies in many lands. A host of new nondenominational missions formed in the last twenty-five years have sent missionaries bent on drawing members from existing churches more than on proclaiming the gospel to unbelievers. Consequently, there is genuine fear that Christianity may be a leaven of disunity in the nation. The missionary gets the larger share of the blame because most agents of disruption are expatriates. This is clearly one of the reasons behind the India government's intensified restrictions on missionaries imposed in 1965. Union is secondary to unity, and unity can be achieved without organic union. It is urgent. May the former mutual recognition, friendship, trust, and cooperation among all missionaries of the Cross be fostered once again.

It is the cultural foreignness of Christianity which is most widely resented, and the missionary is held to be fully responsible for this. An eminent economist who is an expert on Latin America remarked that when one looks at North American missions throughout the whole of Latin America he finds that all the missionaries, ranging from Holiness to Roman Catholic personnel, are propagating United States culture. There are only minor differences dependent upon the particular segment of society out of which the missionary comes. Almost everywhere in Asia and Africa one hears that the Western religion denationalizes, deculturizes, and deracinates converts and makes them alien quasi-Europeans in their own society. There is little need to describe the almost completely Western appearance of Christian organization, cultus, and ministry. In a pioneer mission among a primitive people the superficial external cultural trappings of the foreigner appear exotic and outlandish. Father Dournes writes: "The missioners of the past used to think all the customs of the natives were diabolical; the natives paid them the same compliment. One day I took a visitor in black cassock and beard into a pagan village; afterwards I learned the impression he had given: they thought they had seen the devil himself who everyone knew was black and bearded."[10] But given the veneer of universal cosmopolitan technicological civilization creating a superficial sameness everywhere, the complaints must have more to do with attitudes, values, and relationships than with European-style clothing and transistor radios. The majority of missionaries today are genuinely committed to indigenization or adaptation, but the ministers and laymen in the churches have in the past been thoroughly indoctrinated. They tend to confuse Christianity with European expressions of it. However, it is the missionary whom nationalists blame for the slow progress in indigenization. He cannot take the lead in the process, but he can encourage fellow Christians to make cultural adaptation. Meanwhile, by learning to know the culture, love it, and appreciate its true values he can enhance it in the eyes of Christian nationals. By making friendships and identifying with the people the missionary can gradually change his public image.

The attack against organized Christian religion is in sharp contrast to appreciation, especially by Asian peoples, of Jesus Christ as a spiritual figure, a prophet, and a teacher of ethics. Asia is quite ready to accept Jesus in its own way, but balks at accepting Him as the unique revelation of God, as sole Saviour, and as universal Lord. Many Hindus, Buddhists, and others think that they as Asians better understand the Asian Jesus of the New Testament than do His Western disciples. They agree with Dr. Radhakrishnan, the philosopher ex-president of India, that the history of Christianity is the story of the capture and radical distortion of an Asian religion by the alien and misunderstanding spirit of Europe. Orthodox Christology is thought to be a grave mistake and they seek to free the real Jesus from it. From Ram Mohan Roy, founder of the Bhramo Samaj, to Gandhi many eminent Hindus have venerated Jesus and gained insight, inspiration, and power from Him.

Neo-Hinduism is to a great extent the product of this appropriation of Jesus and His message and the consequent reinterpretation of ancient Hindu doctrines. Swamis write popular lives of Jesus, and His portrait is found in ashrams and muths. Buddhists may regard Jesus as an outstanding example of the Buddha or Bodhisattva ideal, but they have not gone as far as Hindus in appropriating His teaching. This Asian view of Jesus makes

the presentation of Christ as Saviour and Lord more difficult. The point to be made now, however, is that many
persons know Jesus well from their reading of the gospels
and that they believe that the missionaries seldom possess
His spirit and His love. They are repelled by the conscious
or unconscious spiritual pride and arrogance of race and
nation which they think they perceive in the missionary.
Father Roggendorf, the Jesuit apostle to Japanese intellectuals, said in an interview that when rarely some secular
agnostic or atheist comes to Christ it is across the bridge
of friendship. A common love of Jesus could be the basis
of friendship, and in that friendship the missionary might
be able to introduce the Saviour and Lord. Christlikeness
in love and servanthood can lend authenticity to the missionary's words.

Pioneer missionaries of the Protestant societies and the
Roman Catholic missionary congregations knew loneliness, opposition, and even danger. However, on the whole,
throughout the nineteenth and early twentieth centuries
at least, they rode high and easily on the flowing, rising tide
of European power and prestige. Now, excepting in a few
remaining colonies, there is no such power to assist them
and even in those colonies it is now a handicap. The recol-
lection of the old alliance with power is an incubus. There
is a new fear of American nonterritorial economic and political imperialism and colonialism. It is this combination
of a resented memory and a new fear of foreign domina-
tion which plagues the missionary today. The missionary
is the object of the charges and accusations reported in
this chapter because he is in most places the Western presence as well as the Christian presence. He is made a
scapegoat. Dr. Ji Won Yong says with discernment:
"Missionaries of today, without manifesting too obviously
a sense of sacrifice, must carry the scars of the past created

by their 'courageous' predecessors, some of which may seem decorative, but mostly ugly. This is the shadow of the Cross." Moreover, there is greater competition for the minds, hearts, and souls of men by resurgent religions and rampant ideologies than at any time since the advent of our Lord, and the missionary is the target of darts thrown by competitors. Because of suspicion and hostility, even in young sister churches, the missionary career may now prove to be one of cross-bearing. Some of us ought now out of personal experience to understand better Saint Paul's beatings, stonings, perils, and travails.

Our Lord promised His witnessing disciples difficulties and hatreds for His name's sake, since the servant is not above his Master (Matt. 10:16–26). Rejection may be the price of love freely spent. Yet more often love and trust answer love that is patient, unstinted, and not self-seeking. That great medieval missionary to Muslims, Ramon Lull, was known as the Fool of Love. He who would go to the nations today needs must be "a fool of love." But he can count on the companionship of His Lord and the sustaining power of the Holy Spirit. We want the persons whom we meet to think well of us, to accept our sincerity, to trust us. But what others may think is not so important as what Jesus Christ thinks of us who bear His name and Cross.

4

Why the Vocational Crisis?

Numerous missionaries to Burma in recent years repeatedly deferred furloughs in view of the virtual certainty that they could not return once they had left the country. During the past decade some appointees to India, having been refused visas after agonizing months of waiting, have persistently tried and tried again, and have eventually found other assignments elsewhere. Other missionaries have remained at their posts in the midst of the perils of civil war, as in the Congo. There is still plenty of evidence of devotion and steadfastness of a high order in the missionary staff if one looks about. Nevertheless, there are too few volunteers to fill vacancies and to man new posts, and the rate of turnover is high. Almost everywhere one may talk with missionaries he finds persons who are trying to build up excuses into respectable reasons for resigning at the end of the term.

Douglas Sargent reports that there is a cynical statement circulating in some regions to the effect that the modern recruits are either plodders or thinkers. "The plodders plod on while the thinkers are soon thinking up good reasons for returning home."[1] He writes:

If there is one word more than any other that is written across the lives of missionaries, particularly younger ones in the postwar period, it is frustration. The Chinese equivalent for this word is "confusion to the point of suffocation," and as a description of how many have felt and do feel it could hardly be bettered.[2]

A crisis in vocation has been building up steadily during the past fifteen years.

The number of missionaries being sent abroad by the American denominational mission boards which are ecumenically related is decreasing in proportion to the total North American overseas staff. The boards having association with the Division of Overseas Ministries of the National Council of Churches of Christ in 1950 had 64 percent of the total staff; in 1960 only 38 percent; in 1962 about 34 percent; and in 1967 probably nearer 25 percent. The chief reason for the decline, in addition to the expansion of staff by boards and societies not related to the D.O.M., is the long-standing policy of devolution which has involved subsidizing independent churches with men and money in place of the old-style unilateral sending of missionaries. Missionaries are sent in response to requests from churches of Asian and African countries. Therefore, people associated with these mission agencies are not perturbed by the statistics, and, in fact, expect fewer missionaries to be needed in the future. This is a sadly mistaken idea of mission, however, for mission cannot be discharged by participating in interchurch aid alone.

But if this were the only meaning of the downward curve of the graph, the figures could not be used as a barometer of zeal and devotion, as the critics of the ecumenical agencies try to interpret the statistics. (Income and expenditure in contrast to personnel show a steadily ascending line.) Unfortunately, that falling curve also reflects the fact that there are not enough volunteers to meet the demands within the present limited sending operation. Recruitment lags, and there are too many resignations at furlough time. Besides the vocational crisis reflected in these facts other factors are also operative, to be sure: governmental refusal to grant visas; expulsion from China, Burma, and the Sudan; and the elimination of some types of service due to national policy in new nations. However, if the churches were sufficiently committed to sending, displaced missionaries would not so generally have been sent home, but would have been redeployed.

Factors behind the downward curve on the graph of personnel statistics in addition to those just mentioned include the disdain of American youths for overseas mission, the hesitancy of boards to take initiative apart from associated young churches, the steady decline in the number of volunteers, the drying up of the supply of unmarried women career missionaries, the short-term expectation of many volunteers, the uncertainty of young churches about what to do with missionaries, the spread of high expectations for voluntary lay witnessing, and a great deal of frustration among the missionaries.

The largest single lot of missionaries has been eliminated by the restrictive and exclusion policies of certain governments. The slowly grinding mills of attrition have had similar effect, although not so dramatic, where governmental welfare policies in the "Third World" nations aim at the eventual elimination of all private agencies. Many doctors, nurses, teachers, and technical experts in specialized services suspect that their days are numbered although they do not know the date of doomsday. There is little that can be done about adverse governmental action, excepting as Christian citizens and organizations within any country reason with their officers or exert pressure upon them. It would be most unwise to seek either the intervention or influence of foreign powers. Missions can do something themselves, however, to influence government officials if they serve the people selflessly and effectively while they may, and by keeping most scrupulously any contracts and agreements with government which may have been entered upon as the basis for residence permission. The United Mission to Nepal gave a good example in this respect and its contract with the government was renewed for a second period. Naturally, all missionaries should carefully obey all laws and regulations, yet each year there are some who offend by smuggling, breaking exchange regulations, or circumventing certain laws. Self-seeking dishonesty can endanger the whole enterprise.

It is quite a different matter, however, when there is at stake a fundamental question of human rights and Christian principle. Then the missionary must be guided by his conscience and prayer. South Africa, Rhodesia, and Angola have expelled missionaries for defiance of national policy and laws, and such offenses may possibly endanger the tenure of all missionaries. But despite that risk, a firm stand on principle and human rights may be the most effective (and unavoidable) act of Christian witness. It may prove to be for the advancement of the gospel.

Many new nations still lack technically competent personnel in public services and therefore still welcome the cooperation of churches and missions in such fields as health and education. If missionaries can serve in, or cooperate with, government programs without compromise of principle, then such service may convince officials of the genuine desire of the Christians to serve the people without self-interest. When Rajkumari Amrit Kaur was Minister of Health in India the author had an interview with her. She related how she had asked the churches and missions to provide her with Christian doctors and nurses whom she might assign to government hospitals and clinics. This Christian princess and minister of state said that something in addition to scientific knowledge and skill, good equipment, and proper medicine is needed in healing. That ingredient is a love of persons for their own sake that when demonstrated in service makes the patients respond to such care and concern and thus contribute to the process of their own healing. This is something which cannot be taught medical practitioners, but must be caught by contagion from love-motivated persons. She said that Christian doctors and nurses have this quality. But, she continued, all responses from churches and missions were negative. There was insufficient personnel for Christian institutions and none could be spared. A golden opportunity may have been lost.

The missions have always said that they wanted and were ready to meet "felt needs." Whenever governments express such desires, churches and missions may well respond by moving into new paths of service. The India secretary of a major American board reported within the past year, on the basis of interviews with officials, that in addition to greater involvement in higher education, "the Indian government is counting on us to pioneer in meeting some of the peripheral needs," including rehabilitation projects for blind adults, schools for the handicapped, and nurseries for working mothers. Expropriation of institutions and threat of further such takeover by administrative fiat have greatly contributed to missionary frustration. In this situation a word spoken to medical missionaries by participants in a conference sponsored by the Christian Medical Council for Overseas Work may apply to all.[3] It is: Agree that all programs and institutions are expendable, but assume that because of need most of them will not be eliminated; and meanwhile do the best possible job, being prepared to leave behind something of which the missionary can be proud for Christ's sake.

One of the most alarming aspects of the decrease in the missionary staff is the short supply of women career missionaries. They won their place in the mission with great difficulty, but they performed such feats of service that they eventually came to comprise the largest category of American missionaries.[4] American men were generally expected to be married, but single women were traditionally expected to remain unmarried excepting for the few who might marry widowers in the mission. These single women have had a ministry of high honor and glory. They have been willing to take more risks and endure more hardships than married missionaries, and they have usually gone further in identification with the people. For a century and a quarter they were willing in large numbers to forego marriage and family life for the sake of advancing the gospel. But 1962 statistics showed that they, including short-term women workers, formed only 14¼ percent of the staff of the D.O.M., N.C.C.C. related boards.[5] At present few American girls are willing to reduce their chance for marriage by going abroad in their early twenties. It is now the accepted thing in our society not only for girls to marry, but to marry very young. Social conformity seems now to be stronger than the missionary vocation to which our women were formerly so devoted.

It is hard to make up this feminine gap in the missionary

force. Of course, if there is need for the service of foot-
loose celibate missionaries—and there is—then the call
should not be addressed to women only, but to men also.
As Douglas Webster affirms, celibacy in missionary service
is for some persons a gift and not a loss or privation or
handicap.[6] One thing is certain, and that is, if there are
fewer single women missionaries, then the wives will have
to step into the breach and do once again the valiant work
which they used to do in earlier times.

It is significant that while there is a falling off in voca-
tions and a drop-out rate of high proportions in the Roman Catholic diocesan and monastic seminaries, such loss
is far less in the specifically missionary congregations. Also
the societies and boards of the "conservative Evangelicals" receive plenty of applicants, although some of them
are not able to commission and send all well-qualified applicants.

Short-term expectations are not in themselves *per se*
to be deplored. They may be due both to the example of
the Peace Corps and other service agencies and to a desire
for a limited experience as an opportunity to test and
prove one's vocation.[7] The first two years of the professional Doctor of Ministry program at the Divinity School
of the University of Chicago are intended to meet this
same kind of inquiry on the American home front. Through
an exploration of ministry in contemporary urban industrial secular society the student is expected to discover
whether he genuinely has a vocation to professional ministry or to a lay ministry in some other profession or business. A short term abroad can be such a proving ground
for vocation; and, indeed, many of the most effective
missionaries in the younger-age bracket found their vocation in short-term service and volunteered on a career
basis. Extremely valuable service is being given by special-

ists today in short-short-term service, just a few months or a year, usually at their own expense. Doctors and dentists have been more numerous than other experts. The value of what they do in a short time in some field hospital is compounded by the impact they make in the home church when they return. However, it is in a very limited variety of circumstances that short-termers can make much of a contribution. They cannot replace career missionaries. What is dangerous and ultimately frustrating is the hidden short-term expectations of persons who volunteer and are commissioned for career service but who are not genuinely committed in heart and mind. Such persons go with mental reservations, and they think that they can gracefully withdraw at the first furlough on some plausible ground if not content at that time. Such persons are not likely to make the fullest effort at adjustment to the conditions of service and to identification with the people. They belong to that group of "thinkers" seeking a way out from the very beginning. Their discontent and apparently plausible reasons for it stimulate the frustrations of others. Very likely such men and women are due for a shock when they return to the homeland, for there are frustrating experiences in abundance in the parish ministry and in all professions which always have to be viewed in perspective to genuine vocation and be overcome. Having failed to make an honest effort overseas, such people are likely to be doomed to disappointment repeatedly in work at home.

The Missionary Wife

Much missionary frustration appears really to be the wife's discontent or is masked as it. This is partly carried over from the homeland in the case of Americans. Suburbia is full of wives frustrated in their domestic situation, feeling insignificant while husbands engage in important activities in the cities. They seek fulfillment in jobs of their own, or in participating in an endless number of clubs, or in having too many babies in the hope that husbands and other women will see that they really have an important function. Thousands of newly married women and of older women who have reared their families work either because they want a career or want more money than the husband brings home. Being a missionary wife was for a number of decades the only manner in which a woman could fulfill a missionary vocation, and many accepted marriage as the only means of getting to the field. They were appointed "assistant missionaries," but performed such heroic service that eventually they were given full rank. They pioneered in work for women and children and have engaged in every kind of activity other than that for which ordination is necessary. A few churches allow women even to be ordained. Today there are only about half a dozen missions which do not give wives appointment as missionaries but make them mere appendages to husbands.

Nevertheless, during the past two decades the notion has been spreading that the spouse of a male missionary ought to be nothing but a wife, having no responsibility or role of ministry of her own. Worst of all, male missionaries are getting this idea. Half a dozen new appointees have in the last years said to the writer in effect: If I were going into a parish in the United States, the congregation would be hiring me and not my wife; and the parishioners would resent it if my wife were very active in the parish. The people of the churches in which we shall be serving abroad feel the same way about it, they say. But pastors' wives used to do much in parochial affairs, and now

American church members seem more to resent a wife's taking of a wage-paying job than any activities in the parish. Any honest pastor will admit that a wife's quiet, unobtrusive, skillful service and influence in the congregation wins forgiveness for many of his own sins of commission and omission against his parishioners. As to the members of the national churches or non-Christians resenting a married woman's ministry, I have yet to see an instance of it. The place of woman in society has changed drastically. This has been a particularly absurd statement when made with regard to the matriarchal societies of western Africa where women have status, authority, and property; where they have from time immemorial been traders and now have jobs the income from which is at their own disposal.

Examples of male conceit can be multiplied. A British missionary in Africa writes: "The missionary's wife should come to terms with the fact that she is first and last always a wife. She should understand that this is a far more difficult task than being a missionary, and it requires greater understanding than is demanded of her husband. The most difficult thing for the missionary's wife is to let her husband go. At least half our problems on this mission field are caused by the wives who will not untie the apron strings which as much as red tape enmesh the modern missionary."[8] That is so much rubbish. None who knows mission history in depth could write such nonsense. There are some overpossessive women and there are fearful ones who hamper their husbands, but psychological testing and counseling now used in the selection of missionaries can generally eliminate them.

It is a denial of a wife's own missionary vocation and a waste of her talent if she has no outlet for that calling and ability. This denial of ministry is just another instance of male arrogance in subordinating women, a tradition which is stronger in the Church than in secular affairs, despite the teaching of our Lord about the equality of the sexes and the ministry of all disciples. In this time of dreadful, terrifying expectations about the results of the population explosion, a missionary couple ought to set a good example to people with regard to family planning and limitation. If that is done the wife will not be forever tied down with child bearing and care. Especially when servants are available for housework and marketing, the wife has plenty of leisure for work. If she has no other responsibility, makes no friends outside the missionary circle, gets bored with those associations, does not identify with the people and their culture, life will be deadly dull for her. Then she will nag her husband or mope. Many persons tell us that it is usually the wife's insecurity and fear for the welfare of her children which are responsible for the withdrawal of a family. At times this is true, but after a long look at the problem the author concludes that just as often a husband is hiding behind a wife's skirts and is not fully honest about his dominant part in the decision. Let the wife be a missionary.

Frustrations

Many are the reasons for frustration which one hears from missionaries as he travels, as they come into his office for a chat when on furlough, or as they write from the field. Now that the field mission has generally been dissolved, the missionary may say that he or she is the forgotten and voiceless man or woman, having a hearing neither from the national church nor the mission board. But it is significant that in the contrary situation—that anachronism in which the board still makes every decision—the missionary also complains that he has neither voice nor hearing. Now that he no longer is boss, but the servant of a national church, the missionary may say further that he is allowed no initiative. He may claim above all that he is denied opportunity for evangelistic witness, the very thing for which he was commissioned. Again one often hears that young churches do not want missionaries, do not recognize their abilities, and do not use them. It is sometimes asserted that the foreigner is an embarrassment to the church. When hearing such lamentations one often wonders about the person's definition of evangelism, whether he has any imagination and power of initiative, and whether he has gone very far in identification with the people. What does he do with his time? Yet all these matters relate to the basic fact that what is still called the missionary enterprise is no longer in most of its operations still truly missionary to any great extent. It has relatively little to do with direct confrontation with unbelief and nonbelief. A "sending" enterprise has given way to a "lending" operation.

What now exists is largely a system of interchurch aid in which Western churches support with funds and personnel those churches which are the fruits of the earlier missionary efforts. They are now independent and assumed to be sovereign and responsible in their own lands and households of faith. The biggest cause of frustration in this situation is the image which the sent person erroneously holds with respect to himself. Despite everything that he may have been told about changed conditions, a man or woman is all too often apt to hold in mind the outmoded concept of the missionary and to shape his expectations in accord with it. He thinks that he is going out to be a *missionary*, whereas in most cases at this moment he is being sent or lent to be an *ecumenical deacon* or *deaconess,* "serving tables" among the brethren of the national churches. This seems to the author to be equally true of those called "missionary" and those designated as "fraternal worker." All too few accept the reality of their status.

Recognition of the self-responsibility of the young churches began only with the World Missionary Conference of 1910 at Edinburgh, and after the Jerusalem Conference of 1928 devolution of authority from mission to church was rapid. The churches met the severe tests of the World War II period, and their performance, plus nationalistic pressures in new independent countries, hastened the acceptance of their autonomy and authority over their own affairs in their own place. Wholesale admission into membership in the World Council of Churches marked their parity with the older Western churches. Field missions were disbanded. The right to ask for, to refuse, and to assign and control missionaries was accorded to these churches by the boards and societies, although the old order still lingers in some quarters. The national churches are supreme in their own households.

However, Western patterns of church order, ministry, support, and institutions had been imposed upon the young churches by the founding fathers, and the economy of most of them will not sustain such a burden. Excepting for a few countries, including Japan and Taiwan, educated ordained clergy are too few in proportion to the communicant membership, the constituency, and the exploding population. Scarcely a church has been financially able to maintain its denominational structure and institutions. Consequently, despite independence, the churches have been forced to rely heavily on support from abroad both in money and personnel, and the boards and societies have felt obliged to comply.

The whole enterprise has gradually become a gigantic system of interchurch aid with little evangelistic outreach in many places, and it is bogged down in the maintenance of denominational machinery and institutions. The power to give or withhold aid and the demand for an accounting leaves a large measure of hidden control still with the boards, and this irritates leaders of churches. The more sensitivity to its honor and dignity shown by any national church, the less ready has an associated mission board been to act independently anywhere in the whole country where that church exists. This situation has denied freedom and initiative to the Western boards in recent years and limited them largely to meeting requests and acting only in concert with national churches.

There is a variety of factors which contribute to the inability of some national church officers to use missionaries effectively and which contribute to the frustration of the expatriates. The missionary has to take full responsibility for one of the most important factors, namely, that which makes it hard for the national to work with the expatriate—the foreigner's sense of superiority, his aloofness, his lack of love, and his difficulty in exchanging the role of boss for that of servant. Then, in the second place, the young churches were told for over a century that when they were mature the missionaries would get out and go elsewhere, and the churches would be left to manage their own affairs in their own way. Therefore, it is now sometimes thought that the presence of missionaries is the mark of immaturity! Naturally, then, there are nationals who are eager to see the missionaries depart. A very erroneous idea of mission and a highly naïve and unrealistic expectation of the imminent conversion of all mankind lay behind that notion. But the Westerners have only themselves to blame for it.

Moreover, the attitudes of young independent churches toward the founding mission societies are very similar to those of new nations toward the former colonial powers. There was ecclesiastical colonialism in missions, too. Nationalist sensitivity, desire for self-sufficiency, and a passion for getting free from foreign control carry over from civic affairs into the churches and the religious realm. The prevailing sentiment was voiced by a conference at Rajpur on "Foreign Missionaries and the Church in India."[9] Its report spoke of the necessity of both nation and Church to achieve "real independence." The participants recognized the requirement of fellowship and interrelation in the universal Church of Christ, but stated frankly and honestly that the problems facing the Church were the same as those confronting the nation. It asserted:

The problem confronting the Church in India today is to decide the manner in which the coming of foreign missionaries into India to assist the Indian Church in its abiding tasks of proclaiming the gospel and meeting human needs of various kinds should be related to the national situation and the prevailing feeling that a truly autonomous and adult Church, while welcoming the fellowship of Christians from abroad, would not be dependent upon them for carrying on her essential functions.

The Church in India is exercised over the question of how, consistently with her dignity, her independence, and her participation in national purposes and ideals, she can continue to have the advantage of friends and resources from outside.

The report states further that the Indian Church will need some specialists from abroad to "enable her to achieve the larger independence which is her goal." Types include educators and medical personnel along with experts in community projects and rural reconstruction. When these needs can be fulfilled by Indians, then "the Church in India will not need foreign missionaries to assist in her essential work, although it is our hope that we shall always have the opportunity of welcoming into our midst fellow Christians from other lands as an expression of the fellowship of Christians all over the world, even as we hope that Indian Christians will be afforded the opportunity to share in the fellowship of Churches in other countries."

This Indian sentiment can be matched by similar views in almost every other country in Asia and Africa. Thus the Christian Council of Madagascar in 1962 stated that despite progress in training personnel there remained a few posts needed to be filled by expatriates. There are difficulties in such borrowing of personnel, it is stated, because the word "mission" indicates dependence on a foreign country, and "missionary" carries an implied sense of superiority. "This is due," it is said, "to the fact that the old missionaries assumed the character of the chief."[10]

The members of young churches are quite right in striving for independence and self-sufficiency in "essential work." The churches in any place must be The Church there in all its fullness. It is good that they want some fellow Christians from abroad to serve as symbols of the supranational and universal nature of the Church. The fallacy of their thinking is that a national church can be sufficient unto itself at any time, and that a little minority group can at any time say that the task of apostolate has been discharged and that the land in question is exempt from being the object of mission.

Nationalistic reactions to the terms "mission" and "missionary" have brought them into bad repute because of their supposed colonialist implications. The substitute terms used in some quarters reveal the shift from mission to interchurch aid. The Commission on Ecumenical Mission and Relations replaced the Board of Foreign Missions in the United Presbyterian Church in the U.S.A., and that new body introduced the designation "fraternal worker" for members of its staff. The term takes emphasis off mission and places it on interchurch relations. It accurately describes the present situation. The name has to do with *koinonia* and *diakonia* within the body and not with witness to the world. It is not even a good word to use for the ecumenical deacon, because fraternal worker is too much like the fraternal delegate, who is the token of friendly good will who brings greetings to a group, but who does not belong and has no real part in the body. That is exactly the situation in which the complaining expatriate workers say they find themselves. The Christian Council of Madagascar chose for them the name *collaborateur*, and a group in the Congo asked for missionaries to come as *frères-collaborateurs*. Those terms at least suggest actual involvement, but they lack the dimension of mission.

Lending does not replace sending, and the ecumenical deacon is not a substitute for the true missionary. Young churches are striving for self-reliance, and with the help of the mission boards and ecumenical agencies they are training the experts they need. Cooperation, programs of joint action, and church unions can eliminate much of the present wasteful duplication of denominational machinery and the consequent demand for men and money. Lively experiments are taking place in forms of "tentmaking ministry." Large-scale enlistment of laymen in voluntary ministry under the guidance of able professional leadership is above all else the answer to the needs of the national churches. There is every expectation that the boards and societies may confidently expect to extricate personnel and funds from involvement in the present interchurch aid activities and direct them into genuine mission. Until that happens the majority of their staff must be content to be *ecumenical deacons*.

There is now a world-wide base for the Christian mission, and young and older churches together ought to be moving forward imaginatively into this second era of the world mission of the Protestant churches and one in which there will be ever closer relations with Rome in missions. But the first representatives being sent forth from the young churches are being enmeshed in the interchurch aid pattern, and most current thinking about missionaries is in terms of lending servants, not sending missionaries for apostolic witness.[11] One now sometimes hears wild outbursts of frustration from Asian missionaries as well as Western ones.

Since there is one body of Christ in all the world, one hopes that the lending of "deacons" will become a multidirectional exchange of personnel, with workers from the churches of Asia, the Pacific, Africa, and Latin America coming to serve in the Western churches. The tremendous personnel needs of those churches presently inhibit this exchange, because the lending of them to the older churches involves hardship. The Commission on Ecumenical Mission and Relations of the United Presbyterian Church in the U.S.A. has an excellent record of inviting such persons to serve on its executive staff at headquarters. But such ministering brethren ought to be deployed at every level of American church life, not confined to central offices.

The men and women who serve in the diaconate overseas have an office of honor, dignity, and great importance. They are visible personal symbols of the universality, supranationality, and unity of the Church of Christ. Aliens politically and culturally but brethren ecclesiastically, they as members of the body of Christ demonstrate that God really does reconcile diverse people with each other in Christ and that Christians do love one another and bear each other's burdens. They are the transmitters of the heritage of the Church throughout the ages and the helpers of the young churches in their appropriation of it. At the same time they ought to be channels through which new insights of younger churches are given to the older branches for stimulation and growth in knowledge and grace.

Moreover, above everything else those lent persons are each in his place for a special job which requires professional or technical competence to perform that job and to teach nationals how to do it. There is a wide range of assignments in general and specialized education, health services, rural and urban ministry, literature, communications, and the like. It can well be argued that the missionary should never be pastor or administrator in the planting and fostering of new churches, but at a later stage the ecumenical deacon can be assigned to such service by the church he serves. There is a dearth of pastors in most lands, and on the whole educated ministers do not want to serve in rural parishes and out-of-the-way places. Nor do doctors and nurses. The "deacon" or fraternal worker, however, will willingly go into such places. Such service is far more important than the present over-concentration in denominational offices and liaison positions between church and mission board.

If the new appointee faces realistically the fact that he or she is being sent abroad to be an ecumenical deacon or fraternal worker, with understanding of what that really implies, and is fully committed to servanthood in love, then the greatest single cause of frustration will have been removed. Servanthood is not slavery. All members of the body are servants of our Lord and of each other. Love, patience, and identification mark the path of servanthood. As the Archbishop said, those deacons should be prepared to "leave their bones" with the people they serve and yet be ready to be replaced. Nationalistic resentments and misunderstandings can be borne, and for every critic there are two friends. The most difficult thing to bear may be the slowness of the national church members to learn how to use the missionary. It has been heartbreaking to the writer to see some of his best students unused or misused by national churches. Often the national churchman has been less ready than the missionary to surrender the old image of the missionary. However, in most instances love and patience have borne fruit and a post of genuinely important service eventually found.

The best fraternal worker is the man or woman with a powerful missionary vocation. The ecumenical diaconate provides many an outlet for evangelistic zeal if one's concept of evangelism is not too narrow. Institutional service brings contacts with persons of other faiths or no faith. A man is usually not tied to a job for twenty-four hours of the day. If a missionary or fraternal worker does not segregate himself among Christians, the opportunity for encounter, acquaintanceship, and friendship is large. Creative imagination and initiative provide the key. Church leaders may even assign the "deacon" to evangelism in traditional forms.

This is a time of radical change in world society and of transition in world mission. There is confusion and there is excitement. Part of the confusion is the abundant frustration of missionaries. But frustration should not allow us either to deny our calling or to surrender to discouragement. Frustrations are a test of faith and vocation. Perhaps the whole Church is being tested vicariously in the persons of the missionaries. Forewarned and prepared as far as possible, we can meet such circumstances and situations. Let us try creatively to overcome them. Let us love those who try our patience and our temper. Fear not even suffering. Millions of our fellows are suffering just because of the inhumanity of their fellow men, and not because they have dedicated themselves to the apostolate. The present moment is the missionary's time of temptation in the wilderness, not his garden of Gethsemane. The causes of our frustrations are far more a tempter's snare intended to make us fail in our stewardship than they are our passion cup. Our Lord when faced with His cup prayed: "Not what I will, but what thou wilt." May that be the prayer of every missionary and ecumenical deacon or fraternal worker when either frustration or suffering assails.

5

Renewal of Mission

The first stage of the mission of the Protestant churches has ended after three and a half centuries. A second is just beginning, and for modern Roman Catholic missions it is a third one. There is growing expectation of accord and even of cooperation between Protestant and Roman mission agencies in the next period, along with participation by the Orthodox. One can with some reason now talk of "the Christian mission." Not a Western Christendom but a community of churches in nearly every nation on earth is today the base of the new world mission. It is only in its incipient stage. A renewal of mission is urgent. Not fewer missionaries, but more—more than ever were sent before—are required by the magnitude of the challenge. The population explosion is reducing the proportion of Christians to the whole population in most regions. This multiplies the number of persons to whom Christ is to be introduced. It also nullifies most national plans for development, and intensifies human needs which call Christians to ministries of compassion. There are very few countries in Asia, Africa, the Pacific, and Latin America (with respect to Protestants) where the churches of any nation can by themselves with their own resources cope with the challenges of the situation. Just to keep even with the population growth the churches of the former mission lands must, according to Douglas Webster, admit fifteen million members each year, and that is not happening.[1] One-third of the earth's population has never even heard of Jesus Christ. Another third is nominally Christian, and the remaining third has heard something but has not responded.[2]

Another challenge comes from the mushrooming urban industrial centers with their swelling masses of lost, depersonalized people. The secular society which they foster is increasingly indifferent to religion. Cities of Asia can as well be called "post-Hindu" and "post-Buddhist" as those of the West "post-Christian." Those ideologies which Toynbee has called the worship of man in his collective power compete with religions for man's allegiance. Ultimately they destroy freedom and justice. The resurgent Asian religions are seeking encounter with Christians and others as they embark on their foreign mission programs. The Western lands, too, now need Christian missionaries from Asia and Africa, since large segments of the population do not respond to the evangelism of the churches in their midst.

Providing fraternal workers for service in sister churches does not excuse Western churches from sending missionaries. Neither can the young churches of Asia, Africa, the Pacific, and Latin America be excused from sending missionaries on the plea that the local evangelistic task is gigantic and the resources small. A dilemma for world mission is posed by the fact that Western Churches possess large resources while the young churches generally cannot yet even support their parochial and denominational ministry. American churches can support far more men and women overseas. However, they now contribute about 64 percent of the total Protestant mission staff, and further enlargement would be strategically dangerous in view of the popular idea that missionaries are agents of imperialism. Nevertheless, that risk must be taken. Prosperous West Germany might do more, and churches in some other countries certainly can do better. There is pressing need for African, Asian, Pacific, and Latin American missionaries in goodly number and also for North American personnel who are not of the white race. The white face of the mission is not an asset today. Although it may appear that young churches, with few exceptions, cannot afford to send persons well qualified to work beyond their borders, the reflex action of a sending mission might generate the power for every aspect of the church's ministry, as happened in the American churches one hundred fifty years ago.

The Asian churches are sending missionaries, but mission is not yet a spontaneous and powerful movement among many of them. It is still too much stimulated and financed by certain American mission boards, and most of it has been developed as a "lending operation" carried out through the East Asia Christian Conference.[3] Good results are being achieved. It is widely believed that Asian missionaries going to other Asian countries do not carry the disabilities of American and European personnel, since Asian peoples have much in common culturally. But there are violent political antagonisms between some of the countries which must be taken into account, and there are great cultural differences. Any common identity disappears when Asian missionaries live in American missionary residences in an American or quasi-American pattern with allowances upgrading income to the American level. It might well be more effective to employ Asian missionaries in America, Europe, and Africa than in Asia.

It is the conviction of the writer that the American scene needs some genuine missionaries sent out from and supported by African and Asian countries, not just a few fraternal workers on loan for use within existing church structures. The poor in the slums might be more ready to hear the gospel from someone coming out of Indian poverty than from Negro pastors or middle-class whites. An Asian presentation of the gospel might be as attractive to intellectuals as such persons seem to find the teaching of Hindu and Buddhist missionaries. It will be a grave disappointment if, after all the criticism directed against Western mission boards by the young Eastern and African churches, those churches do not come up with radically new and different forms and means of mission and also direct some of their action toward the West. As yet they have shown little imagination and daring.

It is repeatedly stated that there are now more than two hundred Asian missionaries or fraternal workers.[4] This fact—whatever the exact number of such missionaries may be—underscores the truth that the word *missionary* ought no longer to carry the connotation of Westerner, and that all discussion of the role and work of the missionary ought to be about *the* missionary as such, whatever his country of origin. Let the whole Church of Christ now study the problems of sending and the missionary, and not just deal with fraternal workers or ecumenical deacons in the context of lending and receiving.

The World-wide Base

The fact that there is a world-wide base for the world mission ought now to be taken very seriously. This calls for common planning and joint action. But no branch of the Church has the right or power to deny to any other its responsibility for, and initiative in, sending so long as there is an unfinished apostolic task in any country or region. Nevertheless, it is just as true that no sending agency dare ignore existing churches in any area, much less interfere with their ministry. Every church within the Church has the same responsibility. The proposal for Joint Action for Mission set forth at the first meeting of the Division of World Mission and Evangelism at New Delhi in 1961 looked promising.[5] But development of the concept limps along very slowly and uncertainly. Subsequent projects have had more to do with integration of regional church life and work than with encountering unbelief in Christ, and even then the results have been disappointing.

The Sacred Congregation of the Propagation of the Faith has now for three and a half centuries provided overall coordination for the missions of the Church of Rome while leaving to the several missionary congregations, orders, and societies much freedom, initiative, and responsibility. The new directives of the Vatican Council, future reorganization of the Propaganda, and the provision of some form of collegiality seem to offer the mission churches a voice in the enterprise. The Protestant missions need some similar organ, democratically arrived at and maintained, which could provide planning, clearance, and joint action without destroying denominational freedom and responsibility and without still further removing sending from the local congregation or parish.

That is a big order, but it should be attempted. Such an agency could also, through the pooling of funds, remove the national taint from some of the money used in the mission. Any mission agency which desires to launch a new venture in an area where its personnel have not previously been at work should, of course, consult with the churches nearest at hand. Its program should relate to them as far as possible, supplementing them, adding something not yet being done or moving into virgin territory. It should not add still another denomination further to confuse the populace. In many instances the nearest churches might be invited into a program of joint action. The Korea Mission of the Lutheran Church—Missouri Synod, for example, is trying to develop a supplemental program, not a competing one. There are many possibilities for united missions, following the model of the United Mission to Nepal. International, interdenominational, interracial teams and community ministries have scarcely yet been tried.[6]

There are still some areas where the mission is in a pioneering stage—parts of New Guinea, the headwaters of the Amazon, for example—and where genuine mission is still the order. There are other places where there is still fluidity. The missionaries in those places ought to study well and adapt to their situation the principles of Rufus Anderson, John L. Nevius, Roland Allen, and Donald McGavran, avoiding the serious mistakes of earlier times elsewhere. One of the most encouraging developments of recent years has been the emergence of a readiness to foster cultural adaptation especially among primitive peoples in remote places, largely the result of anthropological and linguistic studies by persons associated with the conservative evangelical mission boards and societies. The magazine *Practical Anthropology* is the unmistakable evidence of this happy development. Its issues are filled with valuable illustrations and record the emergence of well-proven principles.[7] It remains to be seen whether or not the missionaries of these agencies generally will have the faith and courage to allow the new Christians as much freedom to develop their own forms of doctrine, polity, and ministry as to make more general cultural adaptations. Patterns become fixed very rapidly, and even in the second generation it is most difficult to foster fluidity and change.

Some Fields for Action

Where should the new missionary drive be directed? First of all, there cannot be too much stress put on the fact that this is the time of transition between the closing stage of the earlier mission and the opening phase of a new era. Bold pioneering and experimentation are the need just now just as in the eighteenth and beginning of the nineteenth centuries. Boards and societies would do well to select a few persons who combine creative imagination and initiative, a warm and contagious faith, and an apostolic urgency to communicate the gospel in a new or seemingly unconventional manner. They should be trusted and allowed sufficient time for experimentation, and certainly should not be required to give an accounting of faithfulness and effectiveness in the form of statistics of conversions. Patience is required of the board as well as of the missionary. The United Church Board for World Ministries has established a category of "missionaries-at-large" who will be "assigned by the UCBWM to function freely within a designated area of responsibility without being integrated within and accountable to a local church and/or mission organization as is normally the case." This action seems to make possible adventurous pioneering.

It would be unwise to try to anticipate where such pioneering may take the churches in mission in the coming decade. But for the moment, while waiting for events and movements to present opportunities, there is merit in looking at some "evangelistic opportunities" on which young churches have reached a consensus. As these situations are examined, the writer gets the impression that the most promising and only adequate approach to each of them is through the voluntary work of laymen in national churches as they are enlisted, inspired, trained, and counseled by expert national professionals and some missionaries working with them.

The reports of the three "Situation Conferences" held under the auspices of the East Asia Christian Conference in Madras, Singapore, and Amagisano, Japan, in February and March 1963, may serve as a sampling of such consensus for our present consideration.[8] The Asian participants in those meetings reported that they found "growing edges" of the churches or new foci of evangelistic opportunity in the increasing Christian diaspora; in the tribal areas of Taiwan, Indonesia, Burma, India, and elsewhere; in ministry to students; in large emigrant groups outside their homelands; in encounter with the resurgent religions; in meeting competing ideologies; in mass communications; and above all in the new urban industrial concentrations all over Asia. Most of this can be duplicated in Africa and some other areas.

Diaspora Peoples

It may have been the example of the fairly spontaneous spreading of Christianity through the dispersion of the Tamil-speaking church members of south India which led the participants in the Situation Conference at Madras to look upon the diffusion of Christians from their home region as an evangelistic opportunity.[9] The cities are draining off the population of the countryside, but that is not what is here in view. Certain Christian communities are on the move. One of the best examples is the dispersion of the Syrian Christians of Kerala in recent years. Both Orthodox and the reformed Mar Thoma members have penetrated to all parts of India, Nepal, and Malaya. They have not only formed their own communities with churches, but they are establishing ashrams and mission centers for evangelism and service among peoples in cultures and with languages thoroughly alien to inhabitants of Kerala. Both church action and individual initiative are involved. The churches are truly engaging in mission; individuals are becoming "nonprofessional missionaries"; and laymen are spontaneously and voluntarily engaging in evangelism. The Bataks have spread through the Indonesian islands and they are said to be the most mobile people there. At home they have been zealously evangelistic. They have been ministering to their own people in the areas of dispersion, and it may be hoped that they will plant the seed of new non-Batak churches. Wherever considerable numbers of church people migrate in this fashion, their home church should endeavor to stimulate them to evangelism. Given apostolic fervor, the diaspora ought to become the means of multiplication of churches as in the first few centuries of the Christian era. This is primarily a field of mission action by the young churches, not Western mission boards. However, when local national churches fail to exploit this opportunity, then the foreign agency might well deploy some missionaries for the purpose.

The large groups of people who emigrated from their homelands in hope of finding economic and social improvement abroad are mentioned as one of the special "growing edges." Here are people more clearly needing missionary involvement than those in the homeland diaspora. There are large populations of Indians in East and South Africa, in the Arabian oil fields, in Fiji, in Malaya, and in the West Indies. The Chinese population in the South Seas and Southeast Asia is by far the largest dispersed people. They form the majority in some places, as in Singapore. Many of these minority peoples are now suffering intense discrimination and even persecution from nationalists in countries where they reside. The vast number of Chinese slaughtered in Indonesia in 1965 will never be calculated within hundreds of thousands, and sheer malice and economic resentment paraded as anticommunism. Christians who participate in such a migration and form part of the continuing new community provide a natural base for evangelism, and some churches, Indian for example, have sent ministers to South Africa and the like for pastoral service. There is a tendency, however, as was the case with European immigrant churches in the United States, for the churches to become vessels for the preservation of the homeland culture and of segregation from national life. Few young churches have had money and personnel to invest in this work, and in some cases mission organizations took the responsibility as an extension of ministry among the parent stock. Some Caribbean Indian churches originated in this manner. In Korea one mission-

ary works among the Chinese. A small Korean church in
Japan is the result of both immigration of Christians and
of missionary action. In Malaya Anglicans and Lutherans
followed up emigrants from India, and Methodists and
others worked with the Chinese. Here the magnitude and
intensity of evangelism among minority groups have been
greater than elsewhere because the government did not
permit mission work among the Muslim Malays.

Churches and missions have a threefold responsibility
toward the large immigrant minorities: to introduce
Christ to them and bring them the gospel, to champion
them against the injustice so widely practiced against
them, and to help them integrate into the national community and its culture. Present mission investment in such
work is a very minute part of the whole world mission
operation, and more missionaries could certainly be employed in this work. There is some reason to believe that
missionaries from an alien culture, that is, alien both to
the minority group and to the nation, may prove more
effective than workers sent from the church in the land of
origin. The latter are too likely to perpetuate the cultural
differences which tie to the homeland and retard amal-
gamation with the land that should speedily become the
new homeland. The missionary from a third culture ought
to be able to take the two cultures, the national situation,
and contemporary social and economic change all into
consideration in the communication of the gospel and the
fostering of churches.

It may be remarked in passing that there appears to be a
kind of crypto-Christian diaspora, a lost, hidden company
of lapsed or unaffiliated persons in Japan. They were converted and baptized while students, but never were integrated into parish life and after graduation disappeared
from view. The conservation of members and the recovery

of the lapsed ordinarily falls within pastoral responsibility, but since in Japan there appears to be very little pastoral concern about this problem the churches ought to make it a matter of special evangelism. Japan is a land where the foreign missionary can work without restriction by government or overt opposition from the populace. A fresh approach by expatriate personnel might discover what has kept these people off the rolls of the local churches and out of Mu-Kyokai, the "No Church Movement." Successful recovery of lost disciples might also bring some light on more effective evangelism to the Japanese in general. One of the most encouraging developments in the Church anywhere is the gradual emergence of zeal and action in evangelism and mission, stimulated by serious study, now being shown by some Japanese churches. Japan has proportionately more ordained ministers than any other country in Asia or Africa and ought to have tremendous potential for mission.

Primitive Peoples

The aboriginal tribes, mostly living in mountain regions or remote places, usually in isolated communities despised and oppressed or neglected by the national majority, are said to be another special and promising field for evangelism and mission. The emergence of the great Batak churches from such a condition, the large and vigorous Karen and other tribal churches of Burma, the rapidly growing Christian communities in New Guinea, and the mass movement among the mountain tribes of Taiwan have focused attention on such peoples. The movement in Taiwan developed spontaneously under the stimulation of a Tyal woman during the war period, and there was no

Chinese or foreign participation until a later time. The Presbyterian Church of Formosa has handled this situation wisely and has fostered self-support and an indigenous ministry. Unfortunately, there has been too much interference by Roman Catholics and some Protestant sects among a people who urgently need to maintain their unity at a time of cultural disintegration, with the hope that having been preserved and not destroyed, they may later undergo a fruitful adaptation to the prevailing Chinese culture of the island.

The greatest numerical success of Christian missions has, with few exceptions, been among primitive peoples. This is not, then, really a summons to new work. However, the swift impact of social change imparts new urgency to the concern. There is argument as to whether the proportionately large investment of men and effort required for mission to small groups, perhaps already doomed to extinction, is justified at a time when nations are trying to integrate such peoples into the national community. It is also said by colonial administrators and leaders of national governments that the provision of a written language and literature perpetuates tribalism and hampers national unity. However, a people respond to the gospel best and most readily through their own language and culture, and it has been found that literacy in the vernacular is an effective aid in achieving literacy in the national language.[10] Recognition of this truth and the work of the missions in line with national objectives has gained for many missions in Central and South America the approval of governments and even their aid. The personal cost to the missionary in ministry to primitive peoples in the more remote places at least is heavy. But every people and every man need Christ. The perilous situation of so many tribal peoples as well as their spiritual state is an urgent challenge to missionary action. One or two decades later the approach to such peoples will be infinitely more difficult. The great obstacle to enlargement of missionary action is now the resentment and suspicion of some governments and many nationalists to what they consider foreign interference with such peoples. The Missionaries' Activities Inquiry Report of the State of Madhya Pradesh in 1956, for example, came out strongly against Christian activity to the tribes. The Indian government has specifically excluded missionaries from portions of Assam. Burma has now expelled all missionaries, and further evangelism among the tribes must be the responsibility of the national Christians. The utmost care and wisdom are required for an enlargement of work with primitive peoples, but the churches should move without delay in the matter.

Students and Intelligentsia

Every ecumenical conference since Edinburgh 1910 and every survey made in the last fifty years has put special emphasis on student work. The Situation Conferences reports are the latest of a long series. It would be hard to find a single place where the student population could today be called a "growing edge" of the churches in that place, but everywhere students do present a major challenge to Christian forces. On the whole, students are nationalistic, anti-Western, devoted to science, agnostic, and skeptical or hostile toward Christianity. New methods are needed. The church school and college still have their role to play, but the focus is shifting from them to governmental and other institutions. The hostel and Christian student center with ample means for encounter can play an even more effective part than the Christian school in reaching the student world at large. There might be added whatever is the local equivalent of the coffee shop, tutoring service, cooperatives, and other activities as needed. The Philippines, for example, have an enormous number of private colleges and universities which are without sufficient full-time faculty members and adequate libraries and laboratories. Few students have the books they need or the opportunity to consult personally with teachers. A union Christian library with staff for consultation and tutoring might make a genuine impact.

Certainly the most effective communication ought to be made from within the student community as Christian faculty members and students create "presence and witness." But the national churches need also a specialized ministry for this work, and they can involve in it many ecumenical deacons or fraternal workers. But the field is large and complex, experimentation is urgent, and there ought to be a place here for the "missionary at large" sent into this situation to work with freedom.

The secularized intelligentsia most certainly form neither a growing edge of the Christian community nor an opportunity for ready harvest, although the Situation Conferences designated them such. They do demand far more serious attention than Protestant churches have ever given them. These devotees of science, technology, cosmopolitan culture, and the quasireligious ideologies regard all religion as rank superstition. They may for family reasons and nationalistic sentiments still participate in some religious rites, but most are agnostic or atheistic. These men and women form an honored elite in most new nations, but few national pastors understand their thought world or speak their language. Roman Catholic missions have regularly assigned a few missionaries to the difficult task of witness to them, but Protestants have usually avoided commitment, preferring the easier contact with the masses.

National churches and missions have two responsibilities toward these intellectuals. One is the raising up of a Christian intellectual elite who can meet these persons on their own ground in voluntary witness. The other is the assignment of capable missionaries to the task of encounter. No course can be marked out for them. They must find the way with patience and imagination. Father Roggendorf at Sophia University in Tokyo stated that there is one point at which the secular intellectual will give religionists a respectful hearing, that is, when they propose solution to a social problem. This re-enforces the conviction of Professor Tillich, of Philip Potter of the D.W.M.E., and most who have been giving guidelines for dialogue—that the dilemma of man and the concrete social problem present the best subject for engagement in encounter. There are two levels on which churches and missions must meet the current quasireligious ideologies: on the popular front and on the level of the intellectual elite. The last is the most important strategically. Father Roggendorf stressed the importance of friendship in ministry to the elite. Few missions will devote much personnel to a ministry which gives so little prospect of a statistical return in conversions. But these persons are of tremendous stature and influence in their societies. Moreover, each is precious in the sight of God. The winning of them for Christ one by one is involved in the discipling of any nation.

Literature and Mass Communications

Literature for the life of the churches and for evangelism has been revolutionized within the past decade and a half. Through the fostering activity of such agencies as the Committee on Christian Literature and World

Literacy literature has become an indigenous product as never before. But there is still a large place for direct missionary participation. In a country closed to direct evangelism and Christian teaching it is imperative. Turkey is the outstanding example here. Mass communications evangelism is a rather mixed bag of programs and devices which vary greatly in effectiveness. It is certainly the opportunity which the Situation Conferences declared it to be. Radio is still the chief medium, but television is challenging. These are costly media in which cooperative effort is essential, and the national churches still need the material assistance and technical advice of Western mission agencies created for that purpose. The fraternal worker has a place of especial importance here in cooperation with nationals, but it is not easy to discern a place for a missionary independent from the churches of a region.

The Metropolis

The three Situation Conferences, the two Asian Conferences on Industrial Evangelism, the All-Africa Urban Consultation at Nairobi, and reports from many lands within the past decade stress the importance of the metropolis for both pastoral care and for communication of the faith. The industrial metropolis is the foremost challenge to the Church in East, West, and everywhere. This is a very new role for Protestant world mission. The cities have been from the beginning the base for Protestant penetration of the countryside and the sites of the biggest local churches, but it was agrarian society which got major attention. With the exception of Japan, missions made most converts in country districts and the majority of churches have been rural. Protestant churches, especially in Africa, have been slow to meet the challenge of the cities. Now it is no longer a matter of facing the city as a concentration of families and individuals, as a cultic, administrative, or commercial center, but as the center of propagation of a new industrial order of society spreading through the countryside and all over the globe. The new secular city has a Christian background in the West and a non-Christian one elsewhere; but it is much the same everywhere, and for the first time mission in America and mission in Eastern and African countries have a common ground and can profit by each other's experience.

It is not surprising that the first special approach to industrial society in the East developed in the industrially most advanced country, Japan. A program of Industrial Evangelism has spread from the Kobe-Osaka-Kyoto area to other parts of Japan and given inspiration to new ministries far and wide in Asia.[11] The Port Harcourt project in Nigeria, the ecumenical program for northeastern India, the urban mission in Bangalore are indications of the growing engagement of the Church with urban society. The studies on "Christian Responsibility in Areas of Rapid Social Change" have stimulated thought and action. Constant migration from the rural districts into the cities and the population explosion increase the magnitude of the task. The other religions, excepting the New Religions of Japan, seem even more uncertain than Christian agencies how to meet the problems.

Hungry for freedom, for human dignity, for better physical living, thousands of farmers flee from the grinding poverty of the countryside into the supposed utopia of the cities. There they do not find the expected paradise, but rather loneliness, hunger, estrangement, and hostility. The new state-managed or sponsored industries need skilled workers, and so do private industries where permitted. But there are few jobs for the unskilled. Housing is scarce and bad. Public service utilities, such as water, sewage, electricity, and transportation, can be neither financed nor expanded rapidly enough to meet the need on even a minimum scale. In the city strangers jostle one another, and few care for their fellow's misery, being lost in their own. Marriage and family life lack the shared responsibilities of rural life, and they disintegrate. Youth has little that is constructive to do. Village church congregations and methods imported into this situation have little positive effect. They do not address themselves to the real situation, to the actual needs of the people, or to the decision-making forces. New patterns of ministry and of Christian community are urgently desired.

A revolutionary new mission to the metropolis is the order of the day. No one denomination or mission can claim on the basis of old comity agreements that it has exclusive right to work in such a place. Not one has the resources for the task. Here is an opportunity for radically new "joint action for mission," not by fitting some bits and pieces of separate denominational programs into a kind of jigsaw puzzle, but by genuine united missions undertaken by national and foreign agencies together. At last there can be concerted action in a unified plan by a wide range of Protestant and Roman Catholic agencies. There are places where there can be a common ministry in many activities, even if separate but noncompetitive local churches are gathered.

Such a program might well start in the rural areas with some orientation to the city being given to people before they migrate. Such persons might be directed to receiving centers in the cities which would aid the new newcomers in their initial adjustment to the new environment. Muslim enclaves in the cities and towns of Ghana are even now performing such a function on a limited scale for newcomers from the Northern Territories, and through such service Islam is growing there. Small companies of ordained and commissioned workers, nationals and foreigners, with a larger company of associated laymen working voluntarily might create informal centers of instruction, service of various kinds, witness, and fellowship. The Indian Christian ashram, if transplanted to the city and its problem of support solved, might offer a model. The members of such a community would need to be such as love people passionately, are biblically and theologically informed, and know something about urban sociology and psychology. Certainly some of them should be trained in social service. All would have to be more selfless than most of us normally are. If Peace Corps volunteers can live in that manner, missionary and national workers should be able to do so too. Some would live and work and earn their own support among the people for the sake of identification, much like the Worker Priests of France. These ministering friends of man would offer Christian love and compassion in the form of counsel, friendship, and practical assistance. The latter might include very simple medicine, especially preventive, adult education, and recreation. There ought to be a new look taken at the old industrial school and an effort made to implement its function in a new manner, fitting many men and women to earn their living by technical crafts now in demand. Small cooperative light industries might be created to employ and train at least some of the vast multitude of now unemployable, unskilled laborers. Such ministry would certainly include organization of the people cooperatively to achieve certain goals by their own effort and others through political action.

The new industrial cities of Asia and Africa have a pagan background or one of an ancient high religion. What few Christian churches are found there may be hampered by inertia, but the vested interests of a long-established old order are not so great an obstacle. There is ground for hope that the present quest for "missionary structures" might more speedily achieve results than in the West and that the engagement with the issues involved in "Confessing the Faith in Asia Today" might bring hopeful guidelines.[12] Asians and Africans are loudly critical of church organization imposed from the West. It is hoped that they will be creative in this urban situation and shape new forms and patterns of community, order, worship, witness, fellowship, and communication. It is also to be hoped that joy and spontaneity would be there along with zeal for evangelism. The activities of the New Religions of Japan may well be studied for clues, because they have spontaneously arisen in the cities and have provided millions of the proletariat with meaning in life, fellowship, recreation, worth-while tasks of service, propagation, reconciliation with their fellows, and communion with the Divine.

It will take a rare new breed of missionary from the West to participate with nationals in such mission in Asia and Africa. But already he is found in the inner cities of the United States and Europe. He is a man or woman who has none of the old missionary pride, who loves unstintedly, and who does not have even an unconscious sense of superiority. In partnership with missionaries and national workers and volunteer laymen of other countries and races he will actually identify with the people in these strange melting pots of traditional culture and the new cosmopolitanism. He will be willing to allow the new community of faith to develop freely under the illumination of the Holy Spirit.

It should be kept in mind that the Church of Christ does not grow and spread in the world primarily by the addition of individuals to the rolls of existing churches. It grows by the multiplication of churches or communities in Christ, even though each person must come to Christ on the basis of his own faith. (This principle does not justify schisms nor the creation of competing local churches.) The new mission should not aim at enlisting individuals in "a Christian movement"—a term popular for several generations in the overseas mission. Mission should be expected under the guidance of the Holy Spirit and by that Spirit's power to result in converts coming together in some concrete manifestation of the body of Christ.

These several foregoing fields of possible action on which there is some consensus by no means exhaust the possibilities of a renewed sending mission to the nations. But they point to possibilities and opportunities for making a beginning. The American missionary must have his part in the renewal and enlargement of mission, and so must the Korean, the Japanese, and the Indonesian. And until the End ushers in the Kingdom of God in all its fullness, the Church in all its separate communities in essential unity must send missionaries as well as engage in local evangelism and lend workers to sister churches.

6

Communicating the Gospel in Dialogue

Both the missionary and fraternal worker or ecumenical deacon have one great new opportunity for communicating the gospel which was not discussed in the previous chapter but left for separate consideration. This is the encounter with the resurgent or revived religions. There is now possibility of meeting on new ground in a changed atmosphere with persons of other faiths in which every "sent one" can discharge his missionary vocation and satisfy his urge to testify for Christ.

Dialogue is the "in" word today. Everybody is for dialogue, both in mission circles and in academic theological quarters. Christians are trying to put off their sinful spiritual pride and infuriating attitude of superiority with respect to each other and persons of other faiths. They are also curbing their tendency to "talk down" to others in unilateral monologue and respectfully and conscientiously to reason with other men in a give-and-take conversation in the course of which there is mutual learning. Dialogue presupposes true communication, not simply announcement or proclamation.

Confessional bodies within Protestantism now engage in dialogue with one another. Roman Catholics, Orthodox, and Protestants talk together in this manner. Christians and Jews meet in common study and discussion, although it is very hard for Orthodox and Conservative Jews to believe that Christians are sincere in view of the terrible persecution of the past centuries. Moreover, there is a consensus through most of the Protestant mission agencies that encounter with persons of other religions should now take this form. The Church of Rome, in Vatican Council II's *Declaration on the Relationship of the Church to Non-Christian Religions*,[1] has also called for dialogue and now has created a special secretariat for non-Christian religions.

Impressive evidence for a true revival of the Asian religions can be assembled, although some Western observers say that all the new activity is merely resurgence and a by-product of independence in many countries of Asia. The writer holds, on the basis of his own observations, that there is a genuine revival. The two most important indications are the intense search for the relevance of religion to contemporary personal and social life and the launching of new missions directed toward Africa, Europe, and America. As for the African religions, there may not be revival, but there certainly is powerful resurgence. Even intellectuals in pursuit of the distinctive and abiding values of negritude are concerned with tribal religion. One marked characteristic of the revival or resurgence is aggressiveness against Christianity. However, despite remembrance of alleged Christian missionary aggression, repression, discrimination, and unfair types of proselytism, all achieved in alliance with imperial or colonial power, there is today throughout Asia a widespread interest in Christianity. There is a readiness of many religionists to talk with Christians who meet them at least halfway.

Dialogue is now even an evangelistic necessity, to put the matter on the lowest ground of sheer practicality. It is in many places the only alternative to a religious "cold war." The militant adherents of other faiths will not today listen to a one-sided proclamation of the gospel, but will listen and discuss with Christians who in turn will give a hearing to the message which those persons believe to be for all men.

The serious threat to all spiritual values and ideals offered by the secular quasireligions of man worship in the form of collective power tends to provide all persons concerned with religion with a community of interest and concerns. Contemporary religious revival collides head-on with a powerful upsurge of secularism. And despite such writers as van Leeuwen, this secularism does not form a kind of Christian encounter with the East, although it does have some Western origins. Much of mankind is indifferent to religion, and a large portion of the remainder are hostile to our faith. They divide into religious and secular antagonists. With both there can be fruitful encounter, but especially with the former because of mutual recognition of the primacy of the spiritual. Any missionary or fraternal worker whose love and humility can be sensed by other persons, who can listen as well as speak, and who is a seeker after truth as well as a witness to truth can find half a dozen opportunities for dialogue in the normal contacts of every day.

The Nature of Dialogue

There are some fundamental facts to keep in mind about dialogue. One is that dialogue is what the participants make it. There are no established forms and rules of procedure. There is not even agreement as to what dialogue is. Academicians tend to consider it their proper domain and want to exclude from participation those who do not belong to the elite of theology and history of religions. Those in missionary circles who are urging such interfaith engagement seem to want only more or less official representatives of the churches or the missions to participate. Some would confine it to the ecumenical Study Centers sponsored by the various National Christian Councils and the Division of World Mission and Evangelism. A learned Muslim historian of religion would exclude all people from dialogue who have a missionary motive. These various types think of dialogue primarily in terms of a structured colloquium, with a panel of experts politely exchanging views. This is the kind of dialogue which is congenial to academicians and much good will comes from it. But dialogue can take place on many levels. Christian students and fellow students of other faiths can talk informally in the universal collegiate "bull session." Any pastor, evangelist, or layman who is theologically literate on even a primary level, who wants both to learn and to testify to the truth in Christ, who likes to converse with fellow men, and who is genuinely friendly can enter into dialogue with any person of like interest he may chance to meet, if they both have leisure for more than a moment's chance encounter. The writer has found that an Indian railway carriage has almost invariably become the place of dialogue, and fruitful dialogue. It is dialogue on this level which can most effectively be the vehicle for Christian witness.

Whatever may be the level or form of the dialogue these following considerations always apply. First of all, systems of religious belief and practice never meet in conversation. It is impossible, for example, for Christianity and Buddhism, or Hinduism and Christianity, ever to confront each other. Only persons who adhere to these religions meet and talk together. The systems of belief and practice are important factors in the meeting, but they have to become incarnate in the persons who live by them before there can be dialogue. Nominal adherence to a religion is no equipment for dialogue, because then the exchange would be no more than a casual and passing exercise in the exchange of views. The authentic note of personal conviction would be lacking. Genuine faith, solid conviction, and religious maturity are prerequisites for encounter.

Secondly, dialogue is not disputation, which is a verbal attempt to conquer a foe. Arrogance and pride always enter into disputation, and real communication becomes difficult. The course of the exchange between Muslims and Christians followed this pattern for centuries, and it has demonstrated how barren and sterile disputation is. Disputants talk past one another, not with each other. Thirdly, dialogue is not the old religious forum, which began with the Parliament of Religions at the Columbian Exposition at Chicago in 1893. In a forum or round table the representatives of religions have been accustomed to analyze, compare, and explain systems of doctrine and to stress the similarities. The end has usually been the depicting of all faiths as varying paths to the summit of the one mountain of truth. Dialogue, on the contrary, recognizes the distinctive differences and contrasts in a common exploration of some subject of real concern to all participants. It involves stimulus and response, give and take, patience and openness, a major effort to understand and to communicate. It calls for an effort to get within the other's heart and mind.

Requirements of Dialogue

Some conditions necessary to genuine dialogue are obvious. They include mutual respect for the other participant as a person and as a man or woman of faith, reverence toward what is sacred to him, and sensitivity toward his mind, spirit, and heart which may not always be able fully to express themselves in words. Some persons who say that there is no continuity between Christianity and other religions, who do not recognize general revelation, and who think that God has revealed His truth only in the Judeo-Christian religion, say that they can engage in dialogue without turning it into disputation; but it is difficult to see how there can be real dialogue unless the Christian believes that God has never left any child of His orphaned, that Christ the Logos has in some measure illumined him, and that the Holy Spirit is with him preparing his heart and mind for the gospel. By God's gift the other man may possess some truth and understanding which the Christian has yet to learn. Other conditions are honesty, openness, and a willingness to learn. Readiness for self-examination is another requirement. Paul Tillich states that a Christian engaged in genuine dialogue is bound to carry on "an internal dialogue" within himself, as he subjects his own position to probing re-examination and fully weighs the views, concepts, and convictions of the other party.[2] Hendrik Kraemer was sometimes heard to say that one never really understood another religion until he felt it pulling and tugging at him, threatening to win him. Tillich says that the internal struggle can be an agonizing experience. Meeting questions never before encountered, having to put answers from a very different position than those traditional in the West, facing new subjects and issues, the Christian must search deeply into aspects of the gospel which he has never seen or neglected, and to explain his faith in radically different ways. This too can be painful, for one may have to change some ideas rather radically. The price of dialogue is great, but the rewards may be great too. They include new knowledge, an enlarged understanding of one's own religion, and a chance to witness relevantly to Christ and the gospel.

One other thing required of the missionary in such encounter with persons of other faiths is constantly to distinguish between the gospel and Christianity. While the gospel is of God, Christianity is to a large extent the humanly fashioned response to the gospel. The chief propounder of the discontinuity between the gospel and other religions, Professor Hendrik Kraemer, has insisted that Christianity is as much under the judgment of the gospel as any other religion.[3] Many who profess to be Kraemer's disciples seem to forget that fact, which is one of his greatest contributions to the preparation for dialogue.

Professor Joseph M. Kitagawa lists four principles as prerequisites for encounter through dialogue.[4] The first is the recognition that each religion is an autonomous expression of religious thought and experience, of necessity viewed in and through itself and its own principles and standards. But all religions have enough in common that a sensitive man of faith can understand something of what another religion means to its faithful followers as he tries earnestly to view its various aspects in their own context. One does not judge the other religion in an alien Christian context, just as the Christian does not want the Buddhist to look at and judge the gospel exclusively from the Buddhist viewpoint. Further, both parties to an encounter should realize that each religion has its own distinctive history and also looks at the history of man from its peculiar perspective. So it follows that no religion can be understood only from the teaching of its founder or a classical formulation of doctrine. The religion must be studied in the totality of its development and in the light of how a particular religious and cultural tradition has conditioned its mode of apprehending the meaning of history and salvation history. Beware then of over-easy comparisons.

Moreover, Kitagawa affirms, one must seek the meaning of another religion as something truly religious, not as just a social phenomenon, for it cannot be discovered by the techniques of social sciences alone. These can help, but the perception of spiritual understanding is essential. Kitagawa, therefore, approves Kraemer's insistence that only persons of serious faith engage in dialogue and be ready to take a self-critical look at their own religion in its empirical form. And lastly, according to this expert in the religions of Asia, a narrow overemphasis on classical doctrine and dogma should be avoided, because a religion is more than a system of doctrine. It is "a community" with beliefs, laws, cultus, customs, and tradition penetrating to the depths of individual, family, and communal life.

It is evident that a missionary's preparation in knowledge, understanding, and attitude should begin long before he goes overseas. He should have a general grounding in the history of religions and a substantial academic introduction to the religions of the region to which he is going. This can be continued after arrival with the aid of the various Christian Institutes for the study of religions at Bangalore, Colombo, Hong Kong, Kyoto, and other places and through their extension services. Now, in constant contact with persons of other faiths in their own cultural setting, he is in a position to make his own critical but sympathetic observations, and he can learn directly from the adherents of those religions. Every missionary who can possibly arrange it ought also to study in institutions or under teachers of the other religions.

Returning to Professor Kitagawa's last point, it may be observed that discussion solely on the terms of classical dogma, Christian and the other, would tend to become academic, abstract, and theoretical, and would involve only the intellectual dimension of religion rather than the totality of faith. It would be likely to deal with problems in terms of outmoded classical models rather than the contemporary meaning of terms and practices. Professor Tillich would go back of the specific doctrines to the establishment of types and contrasting polarities as the ground for dialogue.[5] An example in dialogue in Buddhism is "two telos-formulas can be used: in Christianity the telos of every*one* and everything united in the Kingdom of God; in Buddhism the telos of every*thing* and everyone fulfilled in the Nirvana." But only theologians and philosophers can proceed in this manner. Rank-and-file laymen and run-of-the-mill missionaries can engage in dialogue too, if they can articulate their understanding of their doctrine and its relevant application and are concerned about truth and the problems of men.

Paul Tillich's ground rules for dialogue apply to

scholarly theologians, missionaries, and laymen alike.[6] They are: acknowledgment of one another's earnest conviction, participation only by persons with such conviction who can make the encounter a serious confrontation, the finding of common ground for discussion, and mutual openness to criticism.

Tillich finds contrasting elements in every religion which when paired provide common ground. However, he and Arnold Toynbee both hold that the most fruitful common ground is a joint inquiry on vital issues in the world situation with constant reference to the quasireligions and their secular background.[7] The author's experience in recent years in speaking to audiences and engaging in subsequent discussions in interreligious societies and schools and institutions operated by people of other religions supports this insight. Requests have been mostly for addresses on the bearing of religious truth on the contemporary scene and discussions have centered on specific human problems. It is practically impossible for theistic Christians and nontheistic Theravada Buddhists to get far if they begin initially to discuss the nature or personality of God, for example. The doctrine of man would be a far better subject. But it is best to start with a specific problem of man in the world today, be it in the local community or in the world scene, apply Christian ethics, and then relate this to the Christian doctrines of man and God.

It has been stated that participants in dialogue should be persons of profound faith, firmly holding convictions, but open, humble, and ready for self-criticism. Yet we are all human, and the meeting of persons of opposite views and passionately held convictions presents the dilemma of dialogue. How can it be kept from degenerating into disputation? How is it possible to be open, appreciative, self-critical, ready to learn, and yet present one's own certainties without either becoming or appearing arrogant and intolerant or without getting irritably defensive?

Some suggestions by a Japanese professor are helpful here. Yoshizo Kitamori in an article, "A Theology of Dialogue," in the Spring 1963 number of *Japanese Religions* (Kyoto), contrasts the elements of enthusiasm and tolerance in every religion. Intolerance issues out of enthusiasm, and the indifferent equating of all religions as but varying expressions of truth issues from tolerance. He prefers to call enthusiasm "depth" and tolerance "breadth." It is usually held that depth produces narrowness while breadth results in shallowness. Religion is concerned with truth, and the defense of the truth as one knows it is integral to passionate commitment. The professor argues that religious truth ought to be characterized by a union of depth and breadth. Deeply held convictions need not make a man intolerant and utterly exclusive.

Professor Kitamori takes the doctrine of the Incarnation as an example. This Christian teaching is essentially that God in His love has in Jesus Christ associated Himself in solidarity with man, despite man's self-alienation from God by sin. Mahayana Buddhism's doctrine of Bodhisattva can be viewed in relation to the Incarnation. It teaches that man is not saved individually but only together with other human beings. Thus a sense of solidarity with others is common to both religions. This is a "spirit of breadth." Yet there is a vast difference between the two doctrines. "But," states Kitamori, "if one is deeply committed to this spirit, one's faith can be tolerantly ready to enter into a dialogue with other views while retaining the genuine fervor of its own."

If the Christian will heed Dr. Kraemer's admonition to

keep empirical Christianity under the judgment of the gospel as much as the other religion, if in the discussion he will be the vehicle of the love of Christ for all men, he can keep depth and breadth, conviction and openness, in proper tension and balance. The Golden Rule applies in interreligious encounter as well as in social and economic relationships.

Dialogue presupposes that the participants do not strive for conversion and restrain themselves from any form of coercion and pressure to achieve conversion. Does this mean that the participant may not expect that his witness may lead to conversion or that he may not join in dialogue as a form of evangelism? The academic theologians and historians of religion are clear on this: dialogue may not be a covert form of evangelism. Missionaries are divided on the question. The writer earnestly believes that dialogue is, on the one hand, a form of apostolic witness demanded by the times, and, on the other, that it may be a form of witness to the gospel that is more consistent with the spirit of Christ than many methods of the past. There are excitement and satisfaction in an academic encounter which brings learning and allows for grappling with urgent issues, but the author's concern for dialogue is primarily that it may be an arena for the working of the Holy Spirit. If both parties, or all parties, in the dialogue were zealously committed and convinced of the universal validity of their faith and its teaching, they are more than engaged in a common quest for truth and its application. Each will hope that the truth he knows will so impress the other that it will eventually win his mind and heart. Not being pressed to make a conversion, the Christian engaging in dialogue is not worried about the prestige of his religion and does not have to prove its truth or superiority by winning a conquest. He can play the proper human role in the encounter, and that is to be a witness to the gospel, to introduce Christ, to be himself the manifestation of Christ's love, and to use his abilities to the utmost as the agent of the Great Missionary, the Holy Spirit. He knows that no man can convert another. That is the work of the Holy Spirit, who alone can bring a man to call Christ Lord (1 Cor. 12:3). But the Spirit uses the contagious faith, the conviction, the love, and the relevant witness of the disciple to confront a man with Jesus Christ. When there is actual confrontation with Christ a man cannot be indifferent to Him: he either accepts or rejects Him. That issue can be left to God. The Spirit has worked conversions throughout the centuries, and He will continue to do so. When the Holy Spirit does turn a man to Christ in faith, then the disciple who has become his friend in dialogue will be to him a father in God and a brother in Christ.

7

The Missionary and the Indigenous Church

Mission aims at the planting of new churches into which those who have responded by the prompting of the Holy Spirit to the communication of the gospel are gathered. The most frustrating thing about the missionary enterprise today is that it is primarily supporting existing churches and their related institutions and not producing many new ones.

The agonizing appraisal of the missions to China after 1950 brought to light a number of "lessons" which were supposed to be important for mission work everywhere. Few of these were subsequently acted upon, however. One exception has been the case of the China Inland Mission, now called the Overseas Missionary Fellowship, which as the result of self-study has since in the new phase of its work been stressing the planting of churches in contrast to the earlier, more individualistic goal. Its example has been influential in shaping the policy of other missions in the past, and many of the evangelical missions may now follow in putting as much emphasis on fostering churches in pioneer areas as in winning individuals.

Evangelism as well as sending mission should result in new churches, but never in competition with existing parishes and congregations. The Presbyterian Church in Taiwan has recently given a splendid example. That church set out in the five-year period ending in 1965 to double the membership *and the number of congregations* in celebration of the centennial anniversary of the founding of the church. That goal was reached. The Church of Christ grows by the multiplication of churches, and thus the base of the mission is enlarged.

A new local church when planted should in that place be the body of Christ in all its wholeness. When two or three are gathered together in Jesus' name, He is in their midst. He commissions them to the apostolate, and gives them the Holy Spirit for power in being His witnesses. From the moment of its organization or gathering each church possesses in its own right the spiritual equipment for its total life and ministry. It has the functions of worship, fellowship, nurture and care of souls, ministry of the love of God to men, and communication of the gospel to the world. In order to live, and grow, and discharge these functions that church has to be as much of earth as it is of heaven, to be as local as it is universal.

The gospel is a religion of incarnation. When Christ comes to a people and they accept Him, it is to be expected that He becomes manifest in the transformed lives of individual disciples and in His new community, the Church. The local church is often called a colony of heaven and it is asserted that Christians are called out of the world. But they are called out in order to go back as the body of Christ bearing the message of salvation through the ministry of reconciliation. It is often said that Christianity must always be foreign to this world, but that should not be construed to mean that in Asia it must be an English or German type of foreignness to that place or that in African culture it should be an American Christianity. The new church ought never to be a colony of a planting church in another land and culture, bearing all the marks of the fostering church, and preserving its foreignness in a ghetto of self-segregation.

If the Church is to fulfill its apostolate, the churches in every place must put the message of reconciliation into the language of the people of that place. It must root itself into the culture and society of those people. Only then can it be the agent through whom Christ lifted up will draw all men unto Himself. Only then will it gain the strength needed for its apostolic mission and endure pressure and persecution. Twice the Church was planted in China, but disappeared under persecution because it was not sufficiently indigenous. Then once again it was planted but indigenization was thwarted by the unfortunate Rites Controversy, and the Christian community was rapidly declining when the country was opened by Western imperialistic intervention. A renewal of missionary action was made possible. Now, after a century and a half, the Church in China is in a fourth time of testing, and its fate will be to a great degree determined by whether or not it has become truly indigenous.

It required more than three centuries for Protestant missions to come to a full understanding of what makes an indigenous church. It is imperative that both a missionary going to a pioneer or fluid situation and a fraternal worker going to serve an independent church know something about that story if they are to establish right relationships with the national church. The understanding of this background is necessary to engagement with the fundamental issues in the present.

Protestant missions began in the seventeenth century with Puritan missions to the American Indians and with the work of the chaplains of the Dutch East Indies Company in the Orient. Both missions paternalistically imposed European forms. There were two words always paired in American missionary literature down to the middle of the nineteenth century: "evangelization" and "civilization." There was no argument about the validity and necessity of either, only about the order in which they should be undertaken. Was the acceptance of the gospel first necessary before there could be a desire for civilization and the strength of purpose to achieve it? Or was the attainment of some degree of civilization the indispensable preparation for understanding and accepting the gospel? It was generally held that this was a "chicken-and-egg" question. Each had the effect claimed. Each was considered necessary to the other and to be simultaneously emphasized. They fitted together as hand in glove.

The pioneer missionaries were convinced that European civilization was the fruit of the gospel, especially in the form found in the Protestant North, more especially Great Britain, and the Americans were sure that the gospel had bloomed most beautifully in America. New converts were expected to show the same maturity in faith with the same cultural proofs thereof as Western Christians with fifteen hundred years or more of Christian tradition behind them. They were to manifest Christian faith in the forms of morality, social responsibility, and piety usual in Western Protestant societies. The missions transplanted forms of organization and ministry centered in church buildings and dominated by a paid, professional, educated ministry, both pastoral and administrative. This was all based on monetary support without much questioning of the ability of a society and economy to meet that goal. Professionalization of ministry went even beyond what was usual in Europe and America, because vast numbers of unordained evangelists, teachers, and Bible women were employed. Converts who lost social and economic security upon rejection by families and castes in some regions were employed by the missions and gathered into separate communities around mission stations. There new Christians were isolated and Westernized.

The missionaries expected that there would arise from their efforts as a matter of course an intelligent, Bible-reading, scripture-guided, family-worshiping, church-attending laity, industrious, frugal, and sober, and willingly contributing money to the support of the churches and ministers. Schools and literature were directed toward that end. Along with hospitals they were expected to open doors and create a favorable climate for the hearing of the gospel. Concern about such things as widow-burning, child marriage, foot-binding, temple prostitution, and opium smoking, as well as Christian compassion over disease, poverty, ignorance, superstition, and oppression, made the missionaries social reformers as well as evangelists. All of these things made an impact on the native culture and tended to stress "civilization" of a European nature as a major concern of mission. The missionaries imposed the Western patterns of church organization, cultus, thought, and support firmly upon the emerging churches. This also hampered their growth in responsibility and tended to cut the root of evangelistic zeal in most instances.

However, the pioneers were not engaged in denominational empire building, and most of them believed that denominational differences were the results of European history and without meaning to the peoples of Asia, Africa, and Oceania. They developed a system of comity which was devised, on the one hand, to assure the evangelization of all earth's people and, on the other, to keep denominational differences from causing confusion which might interfere with evangelism.[1] The missionaries were to be pioneer evangelists, not pastors and administrators, and were to get out and go to "regions beyond" as soon as possible. Then the native Christians were to be free to fit the denominational bits and pieces together into a national church which would be different in many respects from any of the planting churches.

Development of the Indigenous Church Ideal

However, the stress on civilization generally hindered rapid evangelization and kept the mission tied to the big central stations. This station system made the missionaries rulers and pastors rather than the pioneer evangelists which they were theoretically to be. By the mid-nineteenth century there were some thousands of converts, but churches were not multiplying, and there was little missionary outreach from the new churches, excepting in the Pacific Islands. Then Rufus Anderson, secretary of the American Board of Commissioners for Foreign Missions, taught that mission was directed toward planting churches and that churches were planted to engage in further mission, both local and foreign. He went to India in 1854–55, broke up the American Congregationalist-Presbyterian central stations, organized village churches, and had pastors ordained over them. His friend, Henry Venn, the great secretary of the Church Missionary Society in London, had been working for the "euthanasia of mission" with result-ant self-government and self-support. The two missionary statesmen in interaction defined the goal of mission as the planting and fostering of churches which would be self-governing, self-supporting, and self-propagating.[2] This for-mula was speedily adopted by most boards and societies, and it eventually provided the foundation for the theory of the indigenous church.

The three-self formula should have been a charter of liberty to the new churches, but during the second half of the nineteenth century the mission agencies in some respects actually worked against it while giving lip service to it. Confessionalism was introduced and denominational colonialism arose. A missionary in India in 1908 could speak, for example, about the prevailing "anxiety lest we should fail to hand on any essential portion of the in-heritance of the Mother Church to the Indian daughter."[3] The fatal "mother-daughter" concept tightened parental apron strings and fixed Western denominational patterns even more firmly on the young churches. When ecclesiasti-cal bodies were created it was the usual practice to make them associations, conferences, presbyteries, dioceses of churches in Europe and America. The missionaries failed to move on to new frontiers, but remained and ruled the churches. While there was talk about the importance of training the native ministry, only a few missionaries actually gave part time to theological education.

Furthermore, as the eschatological outlook of the earlier period gave way to the expectation that the Kingdom of God was being spread through mission institutions of serv-ice, the missionaries put increasing effort into them. They introduced Western education, medicine, and science to the Orient and in lesser degree to Africa, and in so doing made the Christian community all the more Western in character. Little thought was given to the eventual responsibility of the churches for those institutions in their midst. In some instances the missionaries allowed the local churchmen nominal control of the ecclesiastical organization, while they kept control of institutions and evangelism. Missionary institutions were the purveyors of European culture and learning, which many persons wanted avidly for the prospect of economic gain. When in the course of a missionary conference at the end of the nineteenth century a woman asked why the illustrations in curriculum material in the higher schools in India might not be taken from Indian history and culture, rather than entirely from Great Britain, the idea was so startling that none gave her an answer. The missions professed to be seeking the Anderson-Venn goal of independent responsible churches, but for a few decades all too little cultivation was done. Dependent churches were being conformed to the image of "Mother Church," and missionaries ruled them and institutions.

After Edinburgh 1910

The magnificent surveys and inventory of the total Protestant missionary enterprise prepared for the World Missionary Conference at Edinburgh in 1910 brought home to the constituency of the mission societies that there really existed "a native church in the mission field." The child was found to be mature and rebellious under parental control.[4] There was scarcely any evidence of attainment of the Anderson-Venn ideal which all professed to seek. Adjustments in church-mission relationships appeared urgent. The watchword became "devolution," and for the next fifteen years there was stress on the autonomy of the mission churches. But determinative factors in church growth could not be limited to polity, and challenging questions from what were now being called "younger churches" were brought to the Jerusalem Conference in 1928. That Conference opened the way to parity and co-operation, acknowledged the force of the remaining financial controls, and questioned the suitability of Western-style institutions. Moreover, elder and younger churches agreed on a definition of an indigenous church.[5]

A church was defined as indigenous which, while conserving the common heritage of the universal Church, interpreted Christ and expressed its worship and service in cultural forms characteristic of the people. Further, it must bring the spirit of Christ to influence all phases of national life and share its own life with the nation, while courageously contributing to the solution of the problems of the time, and being kindled with missionary ardor. J. Merle Davis, as director of the Department of Social and Economic Counsel of the International Missionary Council in the following years emphasized the role of the mission as an agent of cultural change and stressed the necessity of adapting the local church to the social and economic base of the land. This was called "the fourth dimension" in missions.[6]

The Madras Conference of 1938 adopted a further definition of the indigenous church.

An indigenous church, young or old, in the East or in the West, is a church which, rooted in obedience to Christ, spontaneously uses forms of thought and modes of action natural and familiar in its own environment. . . . Not unmindful of the experiences and teachings which the older churches have recorded in their confessions and liturgies . . . every young church will seek to bear witness to the same Gospel in new tongues. That is, in a direct, clear and close relationship with the cultural and religious heritage of its own country.[7]

The definition further eliminated any wrong ideas of introverted "selfhood" and linked indigenization with apostolate.

If any church is to be truly indigenous, it should adapt its life to its cultural environment socially and economically in organization, forms of ministry, ways of ministry, evangelism, cultus, and means of support. Devotional life, spiritual discipline, literature must take on national garb. Doctrine should be reformulated in thought forms that are meaningful and can get serious attention. Standing within the nation, churchmen should bring the illumination of the gospel upon the issues of national public affairs. In other words, the entire national heritage should be brought under the judgment of the gospel, be refined and transformed in some respects, and be offered to Jesus Christ for His glory and the advancement of the Kingdom. God's ancient gifts in the national heritage are gratefully acknowledged. Some practices may not be able to withstand the judgment of Christ and must die forever as far as the Christian is concerned. Other mores and attitudes can be baptized into the Church, transformed and resurrected, and employed henceforth to the honor of Christ. The Church emerges within the culture from the seed of the gospel brought by the missionary, and that local church which there embodies the universal Church is not a transplant from an alien clime which must be fed and watered from afar. It becomes a sturdy tree, deep-rooted in the life of the land.

It is astounding that it should have taken Protestant missionaries three hundred years to accept the indigenous church ideal. Two factors which inhibited acceptance were the "mother-daughter" concept and the capture of the missionary mind by the colonial mentality which perpetuated paternalism. Another delaying factor was a piecemeal attack on the problem and the confusing of one aspect of indigenity with the whole. The national leadership of the young churches tended to identify the indigenous church with the self-governing church and to contend for independence, freedom from hidden control, and parity with the older churches. Missionaries and mission board executives, on the other hand, because of ever-increasing costs, were prone to equate the indigenous church with the self-supporting one, and they tried to foster that ideal. The generally imposed pattern worked against success. Yet notable efforts along differing lines were made from time to time, including the Batak churches of Sumatra, the Karen Baptist churches in Burma, and Dr. R. A. Jaffray's "ladder method" of support in the Christian and Missionary Alliance churches in Vietnam.[8]

There was far less readiness to identify the indigenous church as the self-propagating church. But John L. Nevius and Roland Allen did this and properly related independence and self-support to evangelism. Nevius' plan for Presbyterian work in Shantung left the convert in his own craft or business and his usual place in society. It encouraged him to be a voluntary, unpaid evangelist.[9] He advocated constant Bible study and rigorous stewardship in combination with voluntary service, and proposed simple and flexible church government. His brethren in Shantung did not follow him, but Presbyterian missionaries in Korea adopted his method with amazing success.

It was on the ground of want of apostolic witness on the part of young churches that Roland Allen attacked the prevailing system of Western patterns, mission control and prolonged tutelage, and a paid professional ministry. Like

Anderson, Allen found in a study of Saint Paul a New Testament model for mission, and the strategy which he proposed is much like that of Anderson.[10] His teaching, reduced to simplest terms, is this: The missionary communicates the gospel, and then when a community is gathered he transmits to these new disciples a simple statement of the faith, the Bible and the gospel, the sacraments, and the principle of ministry. The missionary then stands by as a counseling brother in Christ, and he allows the church to develop in its own way under the guidance and power of the Holy Spirit. The resultant indigenous church is evangelistic by nature, and is self-supporting because it has a voluntary ministry.

There are available many good studies of the growth of churches which can enlighten the missionary and ecumenical deacon. John V. Taylor's *The Growth of the Church in Buganda* is a good example.[11] There are valuable accounts of contemporary efforts to communicate the message in intelligible terms and to make cultural adaptation. It is highly illuminating to compare and contrast the methods of two sensitive, understanding, creative missionaries, such as Father Jacques Dournes with the Jarai of Vietnam and Jacob A. Loewen with the Choco of Panama, the one seeking to shape the church on indigenous lines and the other allowing it to emerge out of the culture under the impact of the gospel.[12] No missionary today needs to go "cold" to a new frontier or into the service of an established church.

Many kinds of churches are described as indigenous. Eugene A. Nida describes four kinds of church in Latin America, and his description applies quite generally elsewhere. They are the mission-directed church in which there is no pretense of indigenity, or of being under national leadership; the "national front" church, which pretends to be indigenous but which missionaries control through figurehead national officers; indigenous churches with varying degrees of mission influence; and the completely indigenous church.[13] Dr. Nida's associate, Dr. William A. Smalley, points out the crucial matter of the relationship of the missionary to church funds, either national or from abroad, in the matter of indigenization.[14] He stresses also the necessity of the truly indigenous church continuing to have some normal, currently functional, and operating process of enculturation as part of its growth.[15] It has been known ever since the time of Rufus Anderson that there can be too many missionaries in one place for the good of the growing church, for they can smother initiative and responsibility by their very presence even if the church should be autonomous. One of the most fascinating instances of church development currently taking place is among the Choco Indians in Panama aided by missionaries who spend only their summer vacations with those people. Professor Loewen, out of that Choco experience, writes that there are five functions which the missionary can profitably fulfill in relation to the church: (1) to deliver a relevant message; (2) to discover the deep-felt needs, "the places where the Spirit is already at work," as a source of "native steam" for development and change; (3) to serve as a catalyst in such development and culture change; (4) to function as a source of alternatives; and (5) to be "a friend of the court." It becomes readily apparent that these functions either place the missionary marginal to church growth or make him only temporarily necessary.[16] The missionary can play this role not only in a new church emerging among primitives, but even in a century-old church already old and tired where he may perhaps be the agent of the Holy Spirit in stimulating renewal.

Indigenity and the Established Churches

Today almost every board, society, and missionary is devoted to the ideal of the indigenous church. Alertness to the issues raises high hopes for the newest churches now coming into being. It is in the long-established churches conformed to Western patterns for generations that the problem is baffling. Opposition to acculturation is much more likely to be by both the leadership and membership of those churches than by missionaries. People equate the gospel with the now long-familiar forms and resist change. The bogie of syncretism is repeatedly raised. However, nationalistic pressures both inside and outside the churches and the hunger of Christian youth for a share in their national cultural heritage stimulate change.

The great difficulty today is the conflict between traditional cultures and the fast-spreading new secular technological civilization found everywhere. All societies are in transition. Indigenization cannot be a mere archaeological exercise or an anthropological reconstruction of a vanishing order. The church in every land must be indigenous in contemporary society, in the culture which actually exists. Neither the national leadership nor the counseling missionary dare shape the church's life with reference to anything but the culture in which the disciples are to make their witness. Father Dournes says that when he shall have transformed the whole of the Jarai religion he will not have done all that is needed. "I shall still be in danger of not really encountering the man who is living—and above all who will be living in the future—in a universe which itself is changing and to which he is not acclimatized."[17]

And he warns: we must not adapt the gospel, but ourselves to the gospel.

The fact that further cultural adaptation is the responsibility and prerogative of the people of the independent churches does not mean that fraternal workers are without powerful influence in the matter. They can stimulate and encourage experimentation. They can describe the experience of the Church through the ages in adapting to new cultures. They can point to examples, good and bad. They can stress the difference between syncretism—deliberate borrowing from other religions items which are alien, contrary, indigestible, apt to distort the faith—and legitimate adaptation to Christian usage. Their genuine appreciation of the local culture can give it a new value in the eyes of Christian nationals. They can also make every effort not to foster retention of American or European customs, attitudes, views, and prejudices as if they were part of the gospel itself.

But there is something still more important. The missionary enterprise is today a vast system of interchurch aid, and the younger churches generally want the lent personnel, the financial subsidies, and the fellowship of the Western churches. There is a strong feeling abroad that conformity to the denominational patterns is the price tag on such gifts. The assistance programs of the world confessional organizations are considered, whether rightly or wrongly, as powerful incentives to "toe the line." Even visits to ecumenical conferences in Europe and America and participation in World Council of Churches programs can wed national leaders more firmly to European traditions—so one hears in Africa. In such circumstances the fraternal worker or ecumenical deacon can make it clear to his national colleagues that, as far as he is concerned, there is no price tag on his services. He can state that the national church possesses full Christian liberty, and that his board or society is committed to supporting indigenization in all particulars. The boards, confessional bodies, and ecumenical organizations can reiterate this and keep on giving after some church does make changes. The major test comes when drastic changes are made in polity, forms of ministry, and doctrinal formulation. Neither the fraternal worker nor the gift of money should ever be a fetter chaining the national church to some Western authority or tradition. They should be free gifts in love.

What will most effectively free the young churches from alleged Western inhibition of radical adaptation is the elimination of the need for heavy financial subsidies and the restraining influence which they exert. The surest means to that end is large-scale development of voluntary lay ministry and witness. The fraternal worker can encourage and work for that goal. The missionary in a pioneer area can make a determined effort to achieve it.

J. Merle Davis used to say with regard to self-support that there already exists enough proven experience in that matter which, if known and acted upon, could lift young churches to new heights of economic stability. It is probably also true with respect to fostering indigenization. Each people has distinctive features, but comparative studies can help attain the desired goal. Yet in the end what will give any church the vitality to endure, root itself in the life of the people, and reach out to them is the grace of God through His Son Jesus Christ present in that local church, His body.

8

The Missionary and His Home Church

The missionary has four relationships to maintain in his apostolic ministry: to God, to the people of the land where he is sent, to the newly emerging or already established church in that land, and to his home church which sends him. To each of these he is servant or minister. We have seen something of contemporary problems and issues involved in the second and third. The most fuzzy and uncertain of the relationships is that of the missionary to his home church. One wonders why missionaries do not feel more frustration about this than about any of the others.

Sending has become very remote from local churches and exceedingly impersonal. During the early decades of the American Board of Commissioners for Foreign Missions there were hundreds of auxiliary missionary societies of men, women, both, and young people in parishes of the Congregational, Presbyterian, and Reformed churches.

They united in town and country auxiliaries. Thousands of ministers and laymen read the *Missionary Herald* next in frequency to the Bible, and they prayed daily for the missionaries. Where would one find a men's missionary society in America today? How much attention to the overseas mission is given in meetings of the Laymen's League or Denominational Men? The average American churchman, male or female, now thinks of a missionary as the employee of a board rather than as his personal representative doing his own work for him. It is a rare parish which has a keen sense of actually sharing in sending missionaries. Where a mission board still has the right to appeal directly to parishes and individual laymen for regular or special support, and when a local congregation may contribute at least the basic salary of a particular missionary, sending is not yet so remote.

Today in most denominations the world mission is only one of a number of good works all balanced against each other in a single central budget. They are all dependent upon an apportionment system and on income through weekly envelopes. Promotion is by a central department which combines a number of interests. The missionary's sending and going is far removed from the average layman. Some mission boards at present are experiencing financial difficulty in part because territorial units above the parish withhold from benevolent contributions more than their just share for their immediate ministries and church extension. That would have been unthinkable fifty years ago.

It is significant that in all the stimulating and even exciting papers of the Studies on the Missionary Structure of the Congregation, with all their references to "going into the world," that world should be the society of the city and nation. There is practically nothing about sending to the nations.[1]

It is easy in light of such facts to understand why many laymen who have remained committed to sending have turned from denominational missions to participation in lay-directed organizations and nondenominational missionary societies. They want to feel involved. But they are a minority. Far more laymen are indifferent, and many are hostile. Large numbers give impersonally just because the denomination includes world mission in its budget.

Amid all the excitement about mission to metropolis, the struggle for civil rights, and the war on poverty, the denominational assemblies pay little more attention to the sending mission than do the parishes. Associations, conferences, dioceses, and the like receive reports of the mission boards and their committees bring in reports on them. Some perfunctory resolutions are passed. A missionary address may be heard. There may even be a "missionary evening" when all missionaries and visiting nationals sit together on the platform. The assembly may like it better when a movie is shown, perhaps more as a travelogue than as encounter with actual mission. It is traditional to nod toward the sending mission, and so it continues to be done. This is a far cry from the era when the overseas mission was the greatest attraction and carried along with it all the other denominational programs. There is mounting concern and even vigorous protest against the war in Vietnam during the year when this book is written; and one would suppose that churchmen would want to be directly involved in a constructive outreach of Christian love into that area. However, the writer has not yet heard one prayer offered in public worship for the evangelical Christians in that land fostered by the Christian and Missionary Alliance or for the Roman Catholics. Nor has a single minister

or layman been found, when asked, who knew that there
was being carried on there a service ministry of large proportions through the National Council of the Churches of
Christ and associated agencies. But thanks be to God that
as long as an official board of world missions exists within
a denomination there is a guarantee that the sending mission will be carried on even in a period of waning concern.
The Propaganda in Rome and the several National Societies for the Propagation of the Faith assure it also in
the Roman Catholic Church. Eventually, the Holy Spirit
will work a revival of commitment.

Relation to the Board

The denomination is to the average missionary or fraternal worker overseas represented by the mission board which
has sent him. He may gripe about that board and com-
plain that he is its forgotten man or woman, and that he
is without a voice at headquarters since the field mission
has generally been abolished.[2] Most boards treat directly
with young churches now, not through intermediary missionaries. Yet the board takes very good care of the missionary and gives him complete economic security while
he serves it. Salaries, theoretically supposed only to cover
living costs on a sacrificial level, have been increasingly
related to the standard of pastors' living standards in the
United States. There are, however, allowances in abundance: cost-of-living additions, children's allowances grad-
uated according to age, educational grants for the children,
furlough study grants, housing, travel, vacation, all medical expenses, and pension. Administratively, the board
takes very good care of its missionaries' physical needs.
Some persons are irked by this paternalism, and others

think that the board might even do better by them. But American missionaries need only compare their material provisions and care with those of European brethren and the national clergy and workers to realize how well off economically they are. After all, self-denial and sacrifice are still supposed to be conditions of missionary service.

Moreover, the board provides more than administrative care. Personal concern is genuine. The writer has been tremendously impressed with the pastoral care of missionaries exercised by almost every area executive with whom he is acquainted. This is even more likely to be true when the area secretary himself has previously been a field missionary. The secretaries spend much time traveling because of the rapidity of change and the urgent necessity of face-to-face consultation with leaders of the national churches. In the course of these travels they normally try to see as many missionaries as possible and thus meet with them far more often than was the case a generation ago. The spiritual welfare, the mental and physical health, the problems and the frustrations of the missionaries are burdens on their hearts. Very few executives in the national churches are pastors to missionaries. This is true even when a church has bishops. The writer can think of only a few who are fathers in God to the missionaries.

The only pastor the average missionary has is his area secretary. No secretary feels that he has adequate time for this work of love and concern, but it is amazing what most of them accomplish. In almost every instance the missionary can be certain that he and his family have a true friend in their secretary, and that they will get more personal attention from him, even though he is based thousands of miles away, than the average American minister gets from his president, bishop, or superintendent.

Missionary preparation is still not adequate either in

orientation or on-the-field training; but the boards are generally giving increasing implementation to their long-avowed allegiance to the ideal of thoroughgoing preparation. Recruiting and selection processes have improved markedly. More missionaries now get at least some preparation.[3] Half a dozen major boards unite in the Missionary Orientation Center at Stony Point, New York, where intensive training is given in mission principles, contemporary issues, linguistics, communication, area studies, and community living. This is all too little, but is a tremendous improvement over what has been customary. The short-term training programs of the Peace Corps prove what can be achieved in an intensive manner in a few months. A few boards put their personnel through longer preparation, as in the Lutheran School of Missions connected with the Lutheran School of Theology at Chicago. Many appointees still have only the benefit of a few weeks in a summer orientation course provided interdenominationally. But most missionaries still have no more preparation than some courses in seminary or Bible school. Moreover, there seems to be no really effective field training program anywhere for missionaries newly arrived in a country overseas combining language study, cultural orientation, and missiology.

However, more and more boards are permitting advanced study by missionaries who want it during furlough periods. But few of them are as yet willing to give a man or woman the time and financial support necessary for a doctoral program, even though the person may be serving in a college or some post where that degree is urgently required to contribute to the upgrading of the institution and meet new government standards. It is of little use to maintain institutions which nationalist critics say are second rate, staffed by ill-trained or professionally incompetent persons. One of the best developments of recent years is the annual conference, seminar, or workshop, where missionaries of a single board on furlough from all fields together get a picture of the total world mission and are challenged to work together on contemporary issues and problems.

The missionary candidate can himself do far more to prepare for service abroad than once was possible. Colleges and universities offer area studies, and even the state universities now offer extensive courses in history of religions. Many now even give instruction in Asian and African languages. Advantage should be taken of these possibilities by those students who are even as much as considering missionary service. A new resource for those who have their professional education and are going into city work abroad is the Urban Training Center for Christian mission at Chicago and similar institutes for encounter with secular industrial society. The wives on the whole do not seem to enter earnestly into some of the training programs, probably because some of them do not regard themselves as missionaries. This is a sad waste of opportunity. During the first term on the field anyone who combines intellectual curiosity with commitment to his ministry can find a useful study course for himself should one not be provided, and in most cases his board will commend and aid him. After his first term the missionary will be in a position to make a furlough year of study carefully tailored to his peculiar needs yield great fruit. He will usually find his mission board ready to assist him to that extent at least, if not to longer study.

The missionary or fraternal worker owes loyalty and honest performance to the board which sends him, cares for him, and makes a heavy financial investment in him. Most boards allow him liberty and prize his inventiveness, initiative, and efforts to experiment creatively. They do not want an obstructionist or one who is a rebel merely for the sake of rebellion. They do not want a missionary to circumvent the board and build up independent support for projects and enterprises which the executives cannot approve and which are in opposition to the wishes of a national church. But most executives certainly do not want a lot of "organization men and women" serving under them. I know of only one major board where some able missionaries have been told: "You have perfect Christian liberty. If you do not like our policies, rules, and practices, you are free to resign." I know of more boards which have supported creative individualists, even "mavericks" of high commitment and achievement, sometimes even for a long trial period and against the disapproval of a national church which disliked nonconformity.

My elder colleague in China thirty and more years ago once said to me: "We missionaries are all generals. There are no privates among us." Since then the missionary has become a servant, not a commander. There has been some consequent tendency for people to become "organization missionaries," but most boards welcome the man or woman who is both servant and creative pioneer innovator. They will not tolerate the man who under pretense of initiative is trying to re-establish the order of the boss. Even in new frontier areas where the missionary is planting and foster-ing the first growth of a new church, there will be im-mediate suspicion of the man who begins to speak of "my evangelists" or "my teachers."

Further, something in addition which the missionary owes his board is frequent, careful reporting. The area sec-retaries travel and observe frequently, but they cannot be everywhere and they cannot linger long in any one place. In this time of rapid change, "missionary intelligence"— as it was called one hundred fifty years ago—is as important as it was in the decade when the very first American missionaries went overseas.

Relationship with Local Congregations

Although the missionary's contact with his sending church is mostly with the mission board, that board of world missions is not the church, but only an agency of it. The missionary should relate directly to the denominational church in its local congregations. The church at every level is the body of the disciples, not the hierarchy or officialdom. The missionary is the servant of the home church not only because he is sent by it to minister the love of Christ and of the brethren to other people but also because he has an essential ministry within its fellowship.

The Protestant world mission used to be a highly personalized enterprise. Committed disciples sent a person of their own number to persons in other places to make known The Person, Jesus Christ. Organization and methods were secondary to persons. The movement spread and was sustained by personal contagion, especially that of the women. For many decades "promotion" by the board or denomination consisted solely in the diffusion of missionary information and the making known of needs. It was the missionary himself or herself who was most important in keeping the movement growing and expanding. His reports and addresses personalized the mission. American churchmen never thought of missions in terms of a nebulous movement a hundred years ago, but always in terms of individual missionaries and individual "native" Christians whose names they learned and who personified for them all the hosts of the nameless. Somehow the sending mission must again become personalized and lose its anonymity. It must overcome its remoteness from the local congregation and disciple, and become again the action of the whole body of Christ in all its members in each place.

The missionary's most difficult job as ministering servant is to stimulate awareness of mission and stimulate participation in it within his home church. More effective Christian education and better promotion by the denominational agencies and especially the world mission board can accomplish a great deal. The denominational mission magazines get progressively fewer in number, and many still being published are deadly dull and their contents seem irrelevant to intelligent church members. *World Encounter* (Lutheran Church in America) is an example of what a good missionary journal can be. The *C.M.S. Newsletter* (Church Missionary Society, London), a four-page leaflet, demonstrates the effectiveness of taking the constituency of the society into wrestling with problems over against mere chronicle and description, especially when presented as if there were no change from half a century ago. On the occasions when the writer gets an opportunity to talk to local parish groups he finds that the puzzles and problems of the emerging new stage of world mission and the perplexities of the transition period excite a considerable portion of the audience. Some boards use conducted tours effectively. Mission boards can take steps to secure more effective teaching of mission in the seminaries and attractive, stimulating continuation of education of parish ministers. They can promote intercession, tie congregations more directly to individual missionaries, and bring many of them more intimately into the commissioning of missionaries. But when all is said, none can do so much to stimulate awareness of mission as the missionary himself.

Douglas Webster has an interesting passage on "Missionary Awareness" in *Local Church and World Mission*.[4] He calls attention to Saint Paul's efforts to make the local church aware of the whole Church, "to widen a church's interests from the parochial to the world-wide." He says that Paul went about this objective in four ways which still apply today. They are: first, by letters, then by people, thirdly by fund-raising, and fourthly by direct reporting. Paul was constantly telling one church about another. His letters to one particular church circulated among many. This was the genesis of the New Testament and of the whole range of missionary literature today.

Letters from missionaries to local churches and to individuals can be one of the most effective means of personalizing mission, making it concrete. Letters stimulate awareness. Most boards provide a letter service for their missionaries, mimeographing a circular letter and sending it to a designated list of persons. Scores of missionaries have their letters sent to the author, and one board sends me a copy of every letter duplicated and distributed. I learn much from these letters but must admit that less than ten percent of them would induce me to give, pray, and work for the mission. How to write letters ought to be part of the instruction of missionaries during orientation and in furlough-time institutes. Letters should take the reader right there into the critical issues in the life of a national church or into the encounter with men of other faiths or of no faith. Much more effective also than a letter sent out from New York, St. Louis, or Chicago is one from abroad bearing a foreign stamp and two sentences of personal message in script added to the circular text, even though three months may be added to transit time.

Paul, says Webster, believed in keeping Christians in

circulation. Today church members are moving about and abroad by the thousands. Some mission boards have gone into the business of arranging conducted tours, and many more try to give assistance to laymen going overseas in hope that they will be Christian witnesses. More and more church members are going as tourists to Africa, Latin America, Asia, and the Pacific islands. The missionary can be a very effective minister to many of these persons, and either as their host or in chance contact can impart to many of them knowledge and insight respecting the country and can introduce them to the church in that land. Missionaries may think this an onerous burden, and they will resent it when, as sometimes happens, after a great effort has been made to entertain and make comfortable certain visitors, those persons return home and tell how the missionaries have an easy time and live off the fat of the land. When the author and his wife resided in Shanghai for a period they sometimes questioned the time invested in such visitors, but now from scores of church members who have traveled I heard expressions of gratitude and appreciation for kindness, hospitality, and enlightenment received from missionaries. If only a few of those to whom the missionary gives time and effort return home as active propagandists for the cause of mission, this ministry has been successful.

But the most important person who circulates among churches is the missionary himself when he returns on furlough or his colleague, the visiting national church leader. When American missionaries first went overseas in 1918 it was expected that they would remain at their posts until death and never return home. However, it was discovered that not only did men and women need furloughs at home for physical, mental, and spiritual renewal, but that their visits among the churches were essential to promotion of the cause. Nothing else can be as effective as a missionary's presence and direct reporting. Nothing, at the same time, can be more destructive of interest and concern than such a visitor who is dull and whose address is full of cliches, irrelevancies, platitudes, and anachronisms.

It is amazing how many missionaries still give the people what it is traditionally held that they want to hear, and what they did want seventy-five years ago. These comprise the worst features of other religions and cultures, rather than the best, tales of hardships, of conversions highly sentimentalized, and romanticized biographical sketches of pious converts. Such speakers seldom have much to say about a world in revolution, nations in confusion and perplexity as they struggle out of colonial status, national churches with myriad problems, and the host of obstacles which are met on all sides. Frequently, misrepresentations of situations or tales which belittle the people and their government get monitored, reported back to the authorities in the nation, and cause resentment in the very place where the missionary hopes to return to communicate the gospel.

Moreover, the audiences in the parishes are not so ignorant about other parts of the world as they once were. Many parishioners have traveled far and wide as tourists or on business. The remainder have seen television documentaries, and regularly they listen to news programs which cover the globe. They resent a biased or slanted report. But when a missionary comes to a church, and effectively personifies to the people their dollars, prayers, and interest devoted to the mission, when he identifies with them as he has tried to identify with the people back in the field, when he reports to them honestly, and above all when he takes them into the problems and perplexities, then there is every probability that there will be a favorable response.

Nothing is more important in missionary visitation than fostering of intercession. The Protestant world mission was launched and sustained more by prayer than by money. Dr. John R. Mott ascribed to a world-wide fellowship of intercession the success of the Edinburgh Conference of 1910 and of each of the following ecumenical missionary conferences. The intercessory World Day of Prayer over the decades has proved to be a very potent instrument for uniting church women in unity for mission. Prayer can keep the entire world-wide Church of Christ in all its parts and individual members in communion across all man-made barriers. This is the only manner in which we in the West are now united with our brethren in China.

When the writer came home from an internment camp in Hong Kong, he was awed, moved, and heartened when in church after church some one came to him and said, "I prayed for you." I once escorted a distinguished Chinese educator to an Episcopal Church where he was to preach. I will never forget the love shining in the rector's face and singing in his voice when he acknowledged the introduction, saying: "I am so glad to meet you! I know you well. Every Thursday during the three years I was in seminary we prayed for you in the intercessions." Most mission boards publish a prayer calendar providing for remembrance in prayer for particular persons and specific subjects each day. The visiting missionary can ask for its faithful use and tell how important the practice really is. He can suggest other names for intercession. Often he might be able to promote an informal intercessory group.

One hopes above all for regular intercessions in the services of worship of each parish church and institutional chapel. My senior colleague whom I previously mentioned used to preach for forty minutes and pray for twenty. Once another missionary asked him what grudge he held against the Eskimos. The old man protested his love for those children of God. "Well," said the other, "I thought that you must hate them, because they are the only people on God's earth for whom you did not pray this morning." Time is limited, and intercessions must be selective, but the whole family of God and selected individuals and groups within it ought always to be remembered before the throne of grace. There is no better form of missionary education than public prayers for the mission, the national churches, and the missionaries. The most Christian of all prayers is that for the coming of the Kingdom and the doing of God's will on earth as it is done in heaven.

As to the remaining method of Saint Paul for stimulating awareness of mission and ecumenical responsibility—fund-raising—the missionary through his personal presentation of the cause has always been one of the best agents. However, few boards or societies will allow him personally to collect funds. His part of necessity has to be the enlistment of pastors and people in participation, the exciting of the people to interest in the whole mission and passionate concern for certain aspects of it. He can leave the actual raising and transmission of funds to parish officers and pastor, if the board and the denominational central stewardship department will allow some ways and means in addition to the present depersonalized system. The congregation simply has to see some of its money going directly to objects of genuine local interest, or eventually concern will wane.

It may often seem to the missionary that responsibility for the personal enlistment of pastors and people in the homeland churches in active participation in world mission is too heavy a burden for him to carry in addition to his field ministry. But this is a part of his servanthood. He is to the home church as to the young church and to the nations the prime symbol of the Church's universality and of God's calling of all peoples.

What Is the Returned Missionary Doing?

The closing of China, Burma, the Sudan, and some other regions to missionary residence and work returned to their homelands some thousands of missionaries. Health and other reasons continuously send back others. They have become pastors, lay ministers, and members in American parishes. What effect on the homeland churches have they induced? Half of their servant ministry had to be laid aside, but if they are dedicated to world mission the other half of their ministry could still be discharged. Have they exercised it? Such persons ought to be sources of light and power for the sending mission. Family illness, government action, or some inescapable cause may send a man or woman back to the homeland church, but, while he may have to resign, he need never retire from actual participation in the sending mission. Every disciple ought to know that he is intended to man a frontline post in a world mission, and the ex-missionary should be keenly aware of it.

9

Between the Times

The missionary stands between the times. This is the main reason why he and the Church are facing perplexities, baffling problems, and frustrations. But this is also why the Christian world mission is now so exciting and full of promise and opportunity. There is today once again adventure in mission as there was in the time of the Apostles, in pioneering periods, and other days of tremendous change and transition. The missionary today stands between the times in various senses of that phrase, all of which have direct and critical bearing on the mission.

The Coming of World History

Firstly, it can be confidently affirmed that the ambassador of the gospel now stands between the age of the separate histories of peoples and regions, on the one hand,

and of world history, on the other. The lesser streams of history in past ages coalesced into ever greater ones involving larger regions and more peoples. But until now peoples have lived within European, Middle Eastern (Islamic and largely Arabic after the eclipse of Christianity severed that region from Europe), South Asian, East Asian, or African history. American history has been but one aspect of European. Europeans are still reluctant to admit that Africa south of the Sahara had any history until the continent was drawn into the European sphere. Now new techniques of recovering and evaluating oral history reveal the error of that viewpoint. Today there is no region or people not affected by others geographically at a far distance. There is planetary interaction among the nations. The truism that the world is now one needs no elaboration.

However, many of our fellow citizens and even fellow churchmen do not recognize that all the once separate streams of history are now merging into a single history of mankind with a planetary society. The separate treasures of once self-contained cultures are now becoming the possessions of all peoples. The new global society will be shaped by influences from all those once separated parts. Consider for a moment how the interaction and cross-fertilization of many cultures, meeting within in the new unity of the Roman Empire around the Mediterranean Sea, produced the ferment out of which Western civilization issued. It may be expected that even more lively ferment will ensue from the interaction of cultural elements in the planetary melting pot. No matter what may henceforth develop culturally, no nation can hereafter live to itself, nor can any people isolate itself for long, as Japan and Korea once attempted and Burma seems to be endeavoring to do today. All now share in a single history, and schools will from now on study world history as one single story.

We Christians believe that God is the Maker and Ruler of history and hold that history is the realm in which He deals with men. Therefore, we should see this development of a single world history as providential. It is to us further evidence that God has indeed given the nations to Jesus Christ to be His heritage. From the distant ages God has been drawing mankind together, leading men toward that reconciled unity with Him, which in humanity will eventually reflect the unity of the Godhead. It is arrogant and a distortion to say, as many do, that no people have a history until they come in large portion to confess Christ as Lord. God has ever been acting among all His children, all nations; and all history may be viewed as being truly salvation history. Christ is the light who illumines every man who has ever come into the world. The ages move toward His coming and then out from Him toward His triumph. The Greek and Chinese discovery of the universe as cosmos, their recognition of mankind as one humanity, the Hebrew contribution of ethical monotheism, the calling of Israel to mission, and God's work among His Chosen People all prepared for Christ and are parts of salvation history.

However, if rightly understood, there is much to commend Bishop Newbigin's statement:

What is happening now . . . is that the people who have no history are being drawn into the history of which the centre is Jesus Christ; and that is the only history. In other words, that which has been static, or at least cyclical, in which the only movement was round and round, life and death, rise and fall—that is being drawn into a movement which is linear and dynamic, which is moving irreversibly and can never be back where it was before. The ferment of change which arises from the impact upon ancient cultures of the Gospel, or at least of that kind of life which has its origin within Christendom, is the force which is giving an irreversible direction to that which was static or merely cyclical. When I say the impact of the Gospel or that kind of life which had its origin within Christendom, I include technology, Western political ideas, Communism—all those things which have come into the eastern world from the West and have their roots in the Christian tradition.[1]

Protestant world mission has drawn much inspiration and renewed dedication and zeal again and again from "discerning the signs of the times." Churchmen have been ready to see God's hand in opening the way for the diffusion of the gospel and the coming of the Kingdom in both cataclysmic events and in large-scale peaceful changes. None in the past has been so momentous and significant as the emergence of one world history. Western forms of our faith are now inadequate for the world. Asian, Pacific, and African contributions to the fashioning of Christianity as the faith for the whole world of men now assume prime importance. And Christianity is not the only religion offering itself as the world religion of the future. Never since the advent of our Lord has there been such fierce and vigorous competition for the minds and hearts of men as is now offered by the old religions, new ones, and the contemporary quasireligions of secularism. Much of the missionary's difficulty and perplexity results from his stand between these two eras of history. He is to many the symbol of resented aspects of the impact of the West which ended the old isolation of peoples and opened the way to one world with a single history. He is still too much the representative of the West in these opening days of one world mission of the Church of Christ to the one world which has come into being. When the missionaries come from all parts of the Church in all lands and go out into all the world, the disabilities now hampering the Western missionary will diminish.

East and West

The missionary also stands betwixt an era of European or Western hegemony over most of the earth and the emergence of some new order. The transition time is marked by bitter revolt against the West, which has not ended with the achievement of independence by numerous nations. It appeared for some years that the outcome might be determined by the result of the struggle between the Western democracies and the Communist bloc. Now that Communist monolith has split. The West is divided between democratic and Communist nations and is faced by the rise and ambitions of a reborn China. Arrayed against both democratic and Communist Western powers there are a large number of new neutral independent nations in apparent chaos and shifting alliances, often called the "Third World" nations. They play the three power blocs against each other while hoping themselves to form a fourth force. Despite their shifting policies, they all unite against the once dominant, imperialist, colonialist West. That was the power structure with which Christianity was long allied in its mission. Now both Western Christianity and its Western missionary pay the price of that historical association.

There is a sense in which it can be argued that the West has won despite the loss of political power and prestige. Douglas Webster says that the evidence is in the potent Western pressures of "Communism, technology, and Hollywood."[2] Competent historians, including Sir George Sansom and Arnold Toynbee, have long documented the thesis that the East willingly accepted European science and technology and what it wanted of philosophical and political ideas, but decisively rejected the religion of the West. Rejection, they say, was partly because of the arrogance and coercion with which Christianity was propagated and partly because Europeans themselves had divorced religion from other aspects of their civilization and personal life. They set the example for selectivity.

However, the mission out of Europe and America was not without great effect. It carried and planted the seeds of revolution at the same time that it planted churches which survive. It was a major transmitter of Western idealism, science, technology, and creativity through its schools. It taught the revolutionary doctrines of individual dignity, freedom, and responsibility. It, too, became a force in the modernizing of the ancient religions and in promoting their resurgence. Yet the impact of Western technology and secularism on Asian and tribal religions is proving to be as catastrophic for them as for the Christian mission. The reader will find a very stimulating and provocative book on the impact of dynamic Western civilization (with its Christian roots) on the East and its religions in *Christianity in World History*, by Arend Th. van Leeuwen.[3] Even though one may not accept the theses and conclusions of the work, it will help the missionary understand the consequences of the Western intrusion into the East and many of its implications, or at least questions, for the Church's mission.

The revolt against the West has written *finis* to most of the old ways and means of operating in mission. The old

charts and blueprints are now useless. The old methods
are obsolete and even hindrances. Many of the perplexities
and problems which are posed by continuing Western pre-
dominance in the mission base and personnel have emerged
in the previous chapters of this book. The missionary walks
unknown paths today. The whole of our efforts to find
new forms, ways, and means for world mission is conditioned by the revolt against the West. Tarred with the
stick of Western origin and support, the American and
European missionary in close partnership with African
and Asian brethren must try to become recognized as the
representative of a supranational universal community of
believers in which peoples of East, West, and the Third
World unite and point the way to their brethren.

Agrarian and Industrial Ages

The sent messenger of the gospel stands, furthermore,
between the ages of agrarian and urban industrial societies.
The face of humanity is undergoing swift and dramatic
alteration. The industrial revolution was supposed to have
occurred in the West in the first half of the nineteenth century, but now it appears as if the developments of those
years were only the opening stage of a transformation of
society just now hitting its stride. The last few decades
have witnessed the emergence of a new and thoroughly
secular society through the stimulation of science and
technology and of organization for their exploitation. The
rest of the world is now caught up in this revolution and is
being carried along at a dizzy pace. Changes effected in
Europe and America in the course of a century and a
half are taking place in Asia and Africa within a decade or
two. Even agriculture is being not just mechanized, but

even industrialized, and the new urban secular cosmopolitan civilization and its disturbing thought ways are penetrating the most remote village. Actually all the many phases of the contemporary revolution come together in the context of the industrial city, and here there come to the ignition point the aroused and then thwarted expectation of the poor, the despised, the hungry, the sick, the oppressed.

The agrarian age was agricultural and religious. The urban age is industrial, secular, and irreligious. Old interests, concerns, and values are being swept away. The centers of decision making have radically changed. Man, educated and proficient in science and technology, now believes himself free, master of his destiny, liberated from the control of nature, kings, priests, and even God. Old concepts of Deity are unintelligible. The terminology and imagery of all religions have been derived from pastoral and agricultural civilizations, from the unpredictable beneficence or destructiveness of nature, and from kingship. These things no longer have much meaning, and their continued use makes religion appear archaic, even anachronistic, and superstitious.

Not only does the sending mission have to face practical consequences of rapid social change in the East and Africa, but also the whole Church in its apostolate is challenged to communicate the gospel to a new man. It is not God who is dead, as some theologians say allegorically, but man who is dead—man as we have known him until today. When there is a society of technical competence and of affluence in America which no longer requires the faithful, honest industry of each individual and there can be serious talk about a guaranteed annual income, the man of the Protestant virtues of faith, piety, sobriety, industry, frugality, has certainly vanished. The word of God must now be communicated to secular man, "come of age," in a new language which Christians have not yet learned. Science and technology divorced from spiritual values and direction already are creating a crisis for the new age. The positive fruits of science productive of human welfare are matched by threats which are also the products or by-products of technology, such as annihilation of the race by an atomic holocaust, a new and more terrible tyranny than any of the past erected on the foundation of modern armaments and mass media controls, and, by no means the least, the population explosion. This crisis by its very nature is very probably a *kairos*, *the* specific *time* for a proclamation of the gospel in a new language.

So it is that standing between these two ages the Church and its missionaries, while not neglecting rural society, must turn from the sending mission's long preoccupation with the countryside and tackle the problems presented by the city.

Western Mission and World Mission

There is still another sense in which the missionary to-day finds himself poised between two distinct times. One is the age of a unilateral sending mission to other parts of the earth from a geographical Christendom, that is, Europe and America, with appendages in Australia, New Zealand, and the white minority in South Africa. The coming age, just now dawning, has resulted partly from the success of mission in the old era and partly from the rise and universal expansion of secular, industrial society, in the West as well as elsewhere. It is an age in which the Church in apostolate finds the entire secular-partially religious world to be a new mission field. This world-wide mission field is to be approached from a base of Christian churches and communities diffused throughout the entire earth. The confrontation of the world with the gospel is to be made everywhere. The lines of mission run out in every direction across a multitude of frontiers among every people. The United States, Britain, Canada, Germany, and Scandinavia are mission fields along with Japan, India, and the Congo. A world-wide church has a world-wide apostolate. Moreover, it is the contemporary insight that every Christian should be engaged in the apostolate, either in evangelism or by being sent to the nations. It is surely the working of Divine Providence that has brought us at this particular hour to the understanding that the Church is not the clergy, with laity as servants, but that the laity and their servant clergy together make up the Church and share the apostolate. The organization, ways, and means of the old era of mission are unsuited and inadequate for the new day when the whole Church is expected to move in mission to the whole world. As long as the missionary in 999 cases out of a thousand is a Westerner and is still enmeshed in the forms and relationships of the old mission out of Western Christendom, he will be hampered at every turn. This is a time for bold experimentation in mission in unity.

The Kingdom Here Now and Coming

This is, then, an age of revolution in mission as much as in the world. The missionary may be perplexed and bewildered as he stands in the midst of such rapid, startling, and radical change. Nevertheless, he stands firm, and he has a frame of reference for dealing with all the problems and perplexities of this, as of every, age of transition. He can stand on the firm rock of faith and of the Great Commission, and there he stands between the times in a more ultimate sense than any of those which we have named. He stands on the rock of the gospel between the time of Christ's earthly ministry, death, and resurrection and the time of His triumph. He is placed with a task to accomplish between our Lord's conquest of sin, death, and the powers of this world on Good Friday-Easter-Pentecost-Ascension and the final End. At the End His Kingdom shall come in all its fullness and God will bring history to the consummation toward which He has been directing it from the beginning. The missionary is both the agent and the symbol of God's purpose.

God is at work in His world, in every passing age judging and redeeming, leading onward toward the fulfillment of His purpose. He has made mankind of one blood or stock to dwell on the face of the earth, and He has called the nations and is gathering men into Christ's Kingdom, which is both coming and already here. The missionary is participating in the making of history because "this gospel of the kingdom will be preached throughout the whole world, as a testimony to all nations, and then the end will come" (Matt. 22:14). No era is final up to the last, and each will pass. In each the gospel is to be communicated in a manner that will get a hearing and response and His love is to be mediated to all persons through Christ's ambassadors.

The servants of reconciliation are charged with proclaiming that God has already reconciled the world to Himself through Christ. They plead with men in every time: "We beseech you on behalf of Christ, be reconciled to God" (1 Cor. 5:20). "For in him all the fullness of God was pleased to dwell, and through him to reconcile to himself all things, whether on earth, or in heaven, making peace by the blood of his cross" (Col. 1:19–20). Not just men, but *all things*, are harmonized in the cross. Divine love has conquered. The victory has been won. Christ has overcome the world (John 17:33). The wall of partition between races, faiths, nations, cultures, sexes has been broken down (Col. 3:11; Eph. 2:11–20). The whole creation now hopefully awaits liberation from its bondage to decay and disunity (Rom. 8:21). As Yves de Montcheuil states: "It is necessary to see, by Faith, the designs of Divine Providence pursuing, by the action of grace, at once in the Church and in the parts of the human race that are still outside of her, one same plan of love and mercy, the reunion into a single Body of the entire saved humanity."[4] At the far end of the preaching of missionaries and evangelists is the assured hope "that at the name of Jesus every knee should bow, in heaven, and on earth, and under the earth, and every tongue confess that Jesus Christ is Lord, to the glory of God the Father" (Phil. 2:10–11).

The Gospel for All Times: the Missionary Message

Christ is Lord and the nations are His heritage. The missionary is sent forth to disciple the nations, teaching them to observe all things that He has commanded. However, Christ comes to the world first as Saviour. The first words of the message of reconciliation are "repent and believe" (Mark 1:15). The ambassador of the Lord is the ambassador of His cross. It is sin that corrupts the world and alienates it from God, and demonic powers of evil contend against Christ's lordship. Man was spiritually created in God's image, but the likeness has been distorted. He has often sought to usurp God's throne, and today in the various secular quasireligions worships his own collective power.

There is no need in the present to argue with men about the reality of evil and sin, although they may reject the terms and quibble about the names by which these realities ought to be called. The race of men is now literally "frightened to death." It knows that the wages of sin is death, and it is impotent in the face of mass sin. Even contemporary man "come of age" sees no way out from under the threat. Neither socio-economic planning nor education are saviours. Many scientists are groping for some ethical guide for the control of the terrible powers which they exercise. The terror coming out of our ghettos—the wages of our collective sin against our brethren—is for the average American citizen even more a dreadful threat than atomic weapons. Air and water pollution, another fruit of our collective sin against God and man, is beginning to strike down our neighbors to right and left and threatening each of us, and we have not the will to repent of our bad stewardship of God's gifts and to move speedily in reformation. We know the wages of so many sins, and yet are impotent before them. Where to turn? The "God is dead" people say that they still have Jesus. If a man looks at Jesus long enough, clearly enough, keenly enough, he will see God. And God even on the cross. There "one man's act of righteousness leads to acquittal and life for all men" (Rom. 5:18).

It is the simple biblical story of how Jesus Christ died for all men that is to be told and to which attestation is to be given by the faith of the preaching disciple and the manifestation of redeemed life in the Christian community—the Church in some form or other. None of the theological explanations of the atonement satisfy many men today. The cross is itself always a scandal and a stumbling block to every generation and can be accepted only by faith. Preachers of the cross should not make it more of a stumbling block by insisting on a particular, and probably in the long run ephemeral, explanation of how it saves and reconciles. Men can only apprehend its meaning by faith in the light of the Holy Spirit when it is proclaimed by faith and demonstrated in the corporate life of the Church.

Looking at the cross some beholders come to understand that it authenticates the Incarnation. God, who became one with us men in the Babe of Bethlehem and the young Carpenter of Nazareth, went with Jesus into death on the cross, sharing our mortality, that ultimate human experience. Somewhere in student days in Europe, in some church long forgotten probably, I saw a painting of the Crucifixion. The shadowy form of the Father was depicted between the body of Jesus and the cross. The same nails went through two pairs of hands. Anthropomorphism in depicting God is wrong, but the painter's insight was right. Because of the cross men have been willing to believe that God shares even death with us, and, sharing death, would be willing even to bear the consequences of our sin.

And looking again at the cross men have recognized the high-water mark of our humanity, the revelation of what man really is in the image of God, his Creator. Love unstinted and outpoured, the same as God Himself. The scholar Muretus became very ill in his poverty and was put into a charity ward in a hospital in Paris. The doctors and their students saw him only as a specimen for study. Standing around his bed they discussed his case in Latin, thinking that he would not understand. One surgeon called him "this worthless creature." The sick man surprised and humbled the group, asking in Latin, "Will you call that man worthless for whom Christ died?" Looking at the cross a man gets a new sense of his own worth in the eyes of God and shame at what he actually is compared with the Man on that tree. The cross convicts both of sin and of worth.

When that conviction has come, then the cross can save from the sin which puts man in the place of God, which makes idols of some of God's creatures and many of man's desires, that does evil to one's brother, that makes man individually and collectively a beast rather than a child of God. When repentance is joined with faith, the miracle of God's grace can be effected. The believer is pulled out of the mire of sin, reunited with the Father, and reborn in the original image in which he was made.

Here is only one instance out of thousands in the course of the world mission, the case of Tokichi Ishii, converted in a Japanese prison in the last months of his earthly life.[5] He had lived a life of crime from childhood and committed several murders. One victim was a Geisha. Her lover, who had quarreled with her, was convicted of the crime and sentenced to death. Ishii, then in prison for some other offense, heard about it and had enough decency not to want some other person to die for his crime. He confessed but was not believed. Tried, he was acquitted. Ishii appealed the verdict and was eventually sentenced to death. The legal process took three years. One day in boredom he picked up a New Testament left by a visiting missionary. He found Jesus' ethic a sincere attempt to lead men to practice virtue, but he was not moved. Later he chanced to read the story of the Passion. The death sentence seemed to him inhuman. Then all unprepared Ishii came upon the words uttered by our Lord on the cross: "Father, forgive them."

Then there followed for Ishii an experience as dramatic as that of Paul on the Damascus road. He wrote:

I stopped: I was stabbed to the heart, as if pierced by a five-inch nail. What did the verse reveal to me? Shall I call it the love of the heart of Christ? Shall I call it his compassion? I do not know what to call it. I only know that with an unspeakably grateful heart, I believed. Through that simple sentence I was led into the whole of Christianity. . . .

I wish to speak now of the greatest favor of all—the power of Christ, which cannot be measured by any of our standards. I have been more than twenty years in prison since I was nineteen years of age, and during that time I have known what it meant to endure suffering, although I have had some pleasant times as well. I have been urged often to repent of my sins. In spite of this, however, I did not repent, but on the contrary became more and more hardened. And then by the power of that one word of Christ's, *Father, forgive them, for they know not what they do,* my unspeakably hardened heart was changed, and I repented of all my crimes. Such power is not in man.[6]

Ishii was a new man from that moment. He grew daily in grace and spiritual stature as he studied the life and teaching of Jesus. His diary recorded his spiritual pilgrimage, and the Buddhist chief chaplain bore witness to his new life. Judges, lawyers, jailors, even the governor of the prison, visited him and found blessing. His last words on the scaffold were:

> My name is defiled,
> My body dies in prison,
> But my soul purified
> Today returns to the City of God.

When confronted and redeemed by the cross the redeemed sinner has usually shown two rather amazing reactions. The wondering exclamation escapes his heart:

"Christ died for *me!*" He is convinced that somehow he
is one with all evil-doers throughout history and that his
very own personal sins had part with those of his forefathers in nailing Jesus to the tree. Then he hears the Cru-
cified One pray for him: "Father, forgive." The second
conviction is even more inexplicable than the first. It is
the certainty that in some mysterious way, solely out of
love and by our Lord's own choosing, He assumes the guilt
of His destroyer and wipes it out.

It is easier in the East and Africa where there is corporate solidarity than in the highly individualistic West for
people to sense instinctively that it is possible for one person to assume and atone for the guilt of another. When
I first visited T'ungchow, near Peking, I heard the story
of a family there. A young man was caught smuggling arms
to the enemy, and was condemned to death. He was the
last male of the family, and the continuity of the ancestral
rites depended on him. His uncle went to the commanding
general and begged for the young man's life, explaining
his importance to the family. He offered to be executed
in his nephew's place. The commander agreed. The old
man was shot. The young man was liberated. He must
surely have felt that he had been redeemed at great cost
and must have gone home with love and reverence for his
uncle. This is but a very feeble human parallel, but it is a
clue to understanding. It is something as *personal* as that
youth's experience which converted sinners have found
in the cross. Love outpoured from the heart of God
evokes an answering love and obedience. Repentance,
faith, forgiveness, reconciliation, transformation follow in
sequence. The convert's life is henceforth an endless celebration of gratitude.

The missionary and the evangelist are charged with discipling the nations. Communities are to be led to re-

pentance and converted also, as well as individuals. The prophets pronounced judgment as to righteousness and wickedness on the nations, including Israel. Our Lord exhorted "Jerusalem" and special groups of men. He dispatched His disciples to the peoples throughout the earth. Paul addressed the whole gentile world. Mission history provides examples of barbarous, cruel, demonic peoples being converted and transformed. The dramatic and radical change in the people of Fiji under the first preaching of the gospel is one such instance. Miss Gordon Cummin described what happened in a single decade.

I often wish that some of the cavillers who are forever sneering at Christian missions could see something of their results in these islands. But first they would have to recall the Fiji of ten years ago, when every man's hand was against his neighbor, and the land had no rest from barbarous intertribal wars, in which the foe, without respect of age, or sex, were looked upon only in the light of so much beef, the prisoners deliberately fattened for the slaughter . . .

Then, further, think of the sick buried alive, the array of widows who were deliberately strangled on the death of any great man, the living victims who were buried beside every post of a chief's new house . . .

Just think of all this, and of the change that has been wrought, . . . Now you may pass from isle to isle, certain to find the same cordial reception by kindly men and women . . . the first sound that greets your ear at dawn, and the last at night, is that of hymn-singing and most fervent worship arising from each dwelling at the hour of family worship.[7]

This is not merely a picture of the effect of "civilizing" of barbarians in a remarkably short period. It is a case of genuine communal repentance, conversion, assurance of forgiveness, and redeemed life in Christ.

Modern missionaries have occasion to repent the sins of their fathers in extracting individuals from their social relationships of caste or community and consigning them to an artificial segregated social existence or of making it necessary for the individual to become an exile from his country. The experience of missions in the communication of the faith to, and fostering churches among, primitive peoples especially has revealed the inescapable relationship between the discipling of individuals and the discipling of nations or communities. Out of such experience Jacob A. Loewen among the Choco Indians, for example, affirms the necessity of addressing the entire community, recognizing the existing patterns of authority and getting the sponsorship of those with authority, appealing first to those who can effectively pass on communication within the tribe, and bringing the challenge of belief and change in behavior to the persons and groups socially capable of making decisions for the whole community.[8] Father Dournes in Vietnam stresses that salvation is a community affair, for it is not just each man or woman, but each and every society with all its characteristics and values that presents matter for salvation. "What one must do, therefore, is to prepare that society until it wants redemption as a whole, rather than detaching from it individual members who will then feel cut off from the group and freed from all responsibility." It is not enough to provide an "incubator" for a few selected Christians, for "the seed must generate in the whole people." The missionary dare not console himself with a few baptisms, but aspire "to the creation of thousands of saints when God wills it."[9] The fact that Western nominally Christian nations in this secular age are far from converted does not negate this truth, although it makes the missionary's task more difficult.

Discipling the Nations

It may seem a far cry from the transformation of a primitive society isolated in the South Pacific or a remote region of Panama to the conversion of contemporary nation states and international society. It may appear ridiculous even to think of the possibility of conversion of men in masses. The population explosion makes the old hope of the conversion of every person on earth seem unrealistic. The state deified and worshiped by devotees of the quasireligion of mystic nationalism is by no means ready to capitulate to Christ and to humble itself in repentance. Nevertheless, the gospel is to the whole world and Christians have been charged to disciple the nations. This may not mean that every citizen of some country is to be converted, but it does mean that all are to be invited to meet Christ and that His light is to be brought to illuminate the whole of national life. The Holy Spirit will work some conversions at least and the ferment of the gospel principles will get to work in national life.

Here is the dilemma of the missionary. He can freely urge individuals to believe and repent; but he, a foreigner, cannot speak directly on national affairs, because he will be accused of subversion and expelled. Moreover, should he be a Westerner as he usually is, the finger of scorn will be pointed at his own nation from which he comes. He himself knows that in these things he is indeed a sinner sent by sinners. But that does not negate the gospel. However, the missionary is concerned with raising up churches whose members can preach the gospel to their fellow citizens and cast its light on national affairs. If he should be an "ecumenical deacon" or fraternal worker serving within a national church, the missionary can help his fellow Christians wrestle with their responsibility as citizens and with the application of the gospel ethic and the doctrine of man to their national life. The Christian community is to demonstrate to the larger community the nature of the common life in Christ.

The reality of God's forgiveness of sins and His reconciliation is intended to be demonstrated to the world of men in the forgiveness which one Christian brother shows toward another, even to seventy times seven (Matt. 18:22; Luke 17:3-4). It is made visible in mutual forgiveness and mutual bearing of one another's burdens in the local body of Christ and in the whole Church spread over the globe. Despite our failures and sin in the Church and the churches, he who looks may find these present there. This is what Church World Service really is as it spends the gifts of American Christians in interchurch aid. One finds it demonstrated even in contentious congregations. Dr. William Stewart, principal of Serampore College until recently, tells of a Muslim in East Pakistan who went to the pastor of a local church noted for its factions, quarrels, and wrangling and asked for baptism. He declared that he had been won for Christ by the reality of the mutual caring which he saw there. The kiss of peace had to precede the Liturgy of the Faithful in the celebration of the Eucharist in the early Church. None could offer the remembrance of our Lord's atoning death and commune with Him in the resurrection feast who had not forgiven his brother and himself sought forgiveness. The community of forgiveness is the household of that Kingdom where Christ already reigns. The quality of its life and love is its most convincing declaration that the Saviour is Lord, and that men and nations do come to God in Him.

The world is the field of the gospel. At one and the

same time it is the object of God's saving grace and the arch-enemy of our Saviour and Lord. God is in this world as much as He is in the Church. Jesus Christ has promised to be present where two or three gather together in His name, and He makes the Church His very body to perform His ministry of healing. But at the same time He is the Light that lightens every man, and He has told us further that we will find Him in the hungry, thirsty, strangers, the naked, the sick, and the prisoners when we minister to them in His name and for His sake (Matt. 25:31 ff). When disciple-servants ministering there in His name find Him, they then make Him visible to others. The Holy Spirit resides in the Church to illumine it and to empower it for its work of witness-making. He is also out in the world preceding the witness, making ready for his testimony. A world in need of redemption from its own powers and principalities of evil and in dire want of reconciliation confronts and challenges the Church in some manner peculiar and distinct in every given age between the times. It is the task and privilege of the Church in any and every period to carry the word of God into the world in a way relevant to that period so that the nations may hear the God in their midst calling them home.

The sword of the gospel cleaves, divides, separates, as God judges and redeems in the engagement (Matt. 10:34; Luke 12:51–53). Some do not believe, but some do. It is God who knows the lines of division and the sentences of judgment. Meanwhile sheep and goats form the one flock of the world until they are separated at the final judgment. The weeds and the wheat grow together until the harvest. Good and bad fish swim together in the sea until the net pulls them in (Matt. 25:31–46; 13:24–30, 36–46). Knowing not when the hour of judgment may be, yet knowing that every hour is that time, the Church in its apostolate goes on from age to age announcing the gospel, communicating the faith, and demonstrating its power.

Meanwhile the disciple is always fighting at Armageddon with his Lord; and Christ, lifted up, is drawing all men to Himself (John 12:32). Repentant believers, forgiven, mystically joined with Christ are being gathered into the Church. And the Church, first fruit of the Kingdom, moves by evangelism and sending back into the world as the herald of the Kingdom. It preaches the gospel throughout the world as a testimony to the nations until the New Age of the Kingdom comes. The meaning of what is being done in any age by the missionary, evangelist, pastor feeding Christ's sheep and lambs, and witnessing disciple derives from the one continuing apostolate of the Church between the two times of Christ Saviour and Christ Lord.

The Nation in the Individual

Father Dournes among the Jarai says that it is not enough to make a people turn from a collective religion to a Christianity which they then live as a community. Their new religion must be to them something personal.[10] Any temptation which the missionary may feel to be slothful in his stewardship or to view his work as of little consequence in light of the distance of the End, any frustrating sense of impotence in discipling the nations, is dispelled because for him both the nation and the ultimate reconciliation of mankind are presented concretely in every single person whom he meets. There is more in the Bible from cover to cover about the salvation of nations than of individuals, but the New Testament reveals that nations come to God in Christ by their individual members one by one, even though those individuals may come in mass. The love of God seeks every one of His children. It is not God's will that one perish (Matt. 18:14). Every prodigal son finds the Father's love awaiting him (Luke 15:11–32). Every lost coin is sought, and the bushes are beaten to find the one lost sheep to add to the ninety-nine safe in the fold (Luke 15:8–10; 15:3–7; Matt. 18:12–14). The Son of Man comes through His disciples seeking and saving the lost (Luke 19:10). Jesus Christ through His witnessing servant continues eating with publicans and sinners. Missionary and ecumenical deacon or fraternal worker are sent by persons to persons as ambassadors of The Person, Jesus Christ, to make Him known as Friend, Saviour, and Lord. It is through the contagion of the love and faith of His disciples that Christ draws men to Himself. There is nothing abstract about the mission to nations that is directed ultimately toward the consummation of history. It is concrete in every personal encounter in which the minister of reconciliation can plead, "We beseech you on behalf of Christ, be reconciled to God."

Notes

CHAPTER 1

1. Ralph E. Dodge, *The Unpopular Missionary*, Westwood, N.J.: Revell, 1964; John Carden, *The Ugly Missionary*, London: Highway Press, 1964; James A. Scherer, *Missionary, Go Home!*, Englewood Cliffs, N.J.: Prentice-Hall, 1964

2. John Calvin, *Institutes of the Christian Religion*, tr. by John Allen, 2 vols., Philadelphia: Presbyterian Board of Education, 1930; vol. 2, p. 641 (Bk. IV. 20. 9)

3. *The Documents of Vatican II*, ed. by Walter M. Abbott, S.J., and Msgr. Joseph Gallagher, New York: Guild Press, America Press, and Association Press, 1966; see *Lumen Gentium*, pp. 14 ff, and *Ad Gentes*, pp. 284 ff

4. The Wheaton Declaration, Congress on the Church's Worldwide Mission, Wheaton, Illinois, April 9–16, in *East Asia Millions*, vol. 74, no. 6, June 1966, pp. 83 ff

5. Thomas Wieser, ed., *Planning for Mission; Working Papers on the New Quest for Missionary Communities*, New York: U. S. Conference for the World Council of Churches, 1966

6. World Council of Churches, Commission on World Mission and Evangelism, *Witness on Six Continents*, London: Edinburgh House Press, 1964, p. 175

7. Douglas N. Sargent, *The Making of a Missionary*, London: Hodder & Stoughton, 1960, pp. 28–30

8. Jacques Dournes, *God Loves the Pagans: a Christian Mission on the Plateaux of Vietnam*, tr. by Rosemary Sheed, New York: Herder and Herder, 1966, p. 13

9. For a review of the history of evangelism in recent times in the European and American churches see Paulus Scharpff, *History of Evangelism*, tr. by Helga B. Henry, Grand Rapids: Eerdmans, 1966

10. W. Dayton Roberts, *Revolution in Evangelism; the Story of Evangelism in Depth in Latin America*, Chicago: Moody Press, 1967. For the theology behind Evangelism in Depth see R. Kenneth Strachan, *The Inescapable Calling*, Grand Rapids: Eerdmans, 1968

11. Lesslie Newbigin, *One Body, One Gospel, One World; the Christian Mission Today*, New York and London: International Missionary Council, 1958, p. 29

12. Wieser, ed., *Planning for Mission*, p. 40

13. Rufus Anderson, *Foreign Missions: Their Relations and Claims*, New York: Scribner, 1869, p. 107

14. Douglas Webster, *What Is a Missionary?*, London: Highway Press, 4th impr., 1958, p. 13

15. Douglas Webster, *Unchanging Mission*, Philadelphia: Fortress Press, 1965, p. 7

CHAPTER 2

1. *Student World*, vol. LVIII, no. 3, serial no. 229, 3d quarter, 1965, "Christian Presence" issue

2. Ronald K. Orchard, *Missions in a Time of Testing*, Philadelphia: Westminster Press, 1964, pp. 163–64

3. For a simple, clear discussion of Christian vocation and missionary vocation see Douglas Webster, *What Is a Missionary?*, pp. 36–39

4. Rufus Anderson, "Ought I to Become a Missionary to the Heathen?," in *To Advance the Gospel: Selections from the Writings of Rufus Anderson*, ed. by R. Pierce Beaver, Grand Rapids: Eerdmans, 1967, pp. 175–84

5. Ibid., and also "On Deciding Early to Become a Missionary to the Heathen," in *To Advance the Gospel*, pp. 185–96

6. Robert E. Speer, "What Constitutes a Missionary Call?," New York: Association Press, 1918, reprinted many times by the Student Volunteer Movement and others

7. Sargent, *The Making of a Missionary*, p. 14

8. Webster, *What Is a Missionary?*, p. 40

9. Sargent, *The Making of a Missionary*, pp. 17, 19

10. R. Pierce Beaver, *Pioneers in Mission*, Grand Rapids: Eerdmans, 1966, pp. 30–31

11. Anderson, *To Advance the Gospel*, see notes 20 and 21

12. Webster, *What Is a Missionary?*, pp. 25–29

13. Sargent, *The Making of a Missionary*, *passim*

14. Ibid., p. 145

15. Stephen Neill, *The Unfinished Task*, London: Edinburgh House Press, Lutterworth Press, 1957, p. 140

16. Dodge, *The Unpopular Missionary*, pp. 138–40

17. James A. Scherer, *Missionary, Go Home!*, pp. 71–72

18. Ji Won Yong, "The Role of the Missionary Today," in *Korea Journal*, January 1, 1967, p. 21

19. Jacob A. and Anne L. Loewen, "Role, Self-Image, and Missionary Communication," in *Practical Anthropology*, vol. 14, no. 4, July–August, 1967, pp. 145–60

20. Quoted by the Rev. Gwenyth Hubble in "The Preparation of Missionaries," p. 1, a preliminary paper (dated April 23, 1962) for the Consultation on the Preparation of Missionaries, Toronto, 1963

21. Jacob A. Loewen, in *Practical Anthropology*, vol. 14, no. 4, July–August, 1967, p. 158

22. Loewen, "Reciprocity in Identification," *Practical Anthropology*, vol. 11, no. 4, July–August, 1964, pp. 145–60

23. Between 1811 and 1850 the Methodists lost by death 30 out of 124 missionaries, and the Basel Mission lost 98 by death between 1828 and 1890

CHAPTER 3

1. On comity see R. Pierce Beaver, *Ecumenical Beginnings in Protestant World Mission: a History of Comity*, New York: Nelson, 1962

2. Sargent, *The Making of a Missionary*, pp. 50–51, 53

3. Dodge, *The Unpopular Missionary*, p. 15

4. E. A. Asamosa, "The Christian Church and African Heritage," in *International Review of Missions*, vol. 44, no. 4, 1955, p. 300

5. Loewen, in *Practical Anthropology*, vol. 11, no. 4, p. 152

6. Scherer, *Missionary, Go Home!*, pp. 72–73

7. Carden, *The Ugly Missionary*, pp. 5–6

8. Madhya Pradesh, Christian Missionary Activities Enquiry Committee, *Report*, 2 vols. in 3 parts, Nagpur: Gov't. Print., 1956, the "Niyogi Report"

9. R. Pierce Beaver, *Envoys of Peace. The Peace Witness in the Christian World Mission*, Grand Rapids: Eerdmans, 1964; pp. 50–51

10. Dournes, *God Loves the Pagans*, p. 17

CHAPTER 4

1. Sargent, *The Making of a Missionary*, p. 127

2. Ibid., p. 126

3. At Arden House, Harriman, N.Y., June 5–7, 1963. A useful statement, "Premises of Medical Missions," was published in Missionary Research Library, *Occasional Bulletin*, vol. XIV, no. 10, Oct. 1963

4. R. Pierce Beaver, *All Loves Excelling: American Protestant Women in World Mission*, Grand Rapids: Eerdmans, 1968

5. Based on statistics in Missionary Research Library, *North American Protestant Foreign Mission Agencies*, 5th ed., 1962, New York: M.R.L., 1962

6. Webster, *What Is a Missionary?*, p. 43

7. "This lack of a clear-cut image of the missionary today may at least partly explain the present preference of many young Christians for secular fields of service abroad or for short-term appointments in the service of Christian agencies." Commission on World Mission and Evangelism, W.C.C., *Statement from a Consultation on the Preparation of Missionaries*, Toronto, 1963, p. 3

8. Consultation on the Preparation of Missionaries, Toronto, 1963, "Preparatory Paper No. 5," September 1962, p. 3

9. "Foreign Missionaries and the Church in India," a leaflet, printed at the Lucknow Publishing House, *ca.* 1959

10. Consultation on the Preparation of Missionaries, Toronto, 1963, "Preparatory Paper No. 11," 1962, p. 1

11. All the discussions and findings of the 1963 Toronto Consultation were in the context of cooperation between sending and receiving churches.

CHAPTER 5

1. Douglas Webster, *Local Church and World Mission*, New York: Seabury Press, 1964, p. 17

2. Webster, *Into All the World*, London: SPCK, 1958, pp. 69–70

3. The *Report of Consultation on Asian Missionaries*, sponsored by the East Asia Christian Conference, Bangkok, February 18–22, 1964, begins with an excellent statement on "The Missionary Task," but then treats the subject in terms of "sending and receiving"—once again the ecumenical diaconate only. Only seven out of twenty-five participants listed were actually Asian missionaries.

4. For a survey see "Missionaries from the Younger Churches," by Clara E. Orr, in Missionary Research Library, *Occasional Bulletin*, vol. XIII, no. 1, January 1962

5. World Council of Churches, Commission on World Mission and Evangelism, *Joint Action for Mission*, Geneva: W.C.C., 1962, pamphlet

6. Ronald K. Orchard, *Out of Every Nation, A Discussion of the Internationalizing of Mission*, London: SCM Press, 1959

7. *Practical Anthropology*, William A. Smalley, ed.; Eugene A. Nida, assoc. ed., Box 307, Tarrytown, N.Y. 10591

8. East Asia Christian Conference, *Reports of Situation Conferences* (February–March, 1963), printed by E.A.C.C. and distributed by W.C.C.

9. See N. C. Sargent, *Dispersion of the Tamil Church*, Madras: Indian S.P.C.K., 1940; rev. ed., 1962

10. Loewen, "Language: Vernacular, Trade, or National?", *Practical Anthropology*, vol. 12, no. 3, May–June 1965, pp. 97–106

11. *Church Labor Letter*

12. East Asia Christian Conference, *Structures for a Missionary Congregation, The Shape of the Christian Community in Asia Today*, ed. by John R. Fleming and Kenyon Wright, Singapore: E.A.C.C., 1964; "Confessing the Faith in Asia Today" (20 papers preparatory to the E.A.C.C. Faith and Order Consultation, Hong Kong, 1966), *The South East Asia Journal of Theology*, vol. 8, nos. 1 and 2 combined, July/October 1966, whole issue; E.A.C.C., Faith and Order Consultation, Hong Kong, 1966, *Confessing the Faith in Asia Today*, Report of the Consultation, printed in Australia, available from E.A.C.C. office, Bangkok, Thailand.

CHAPTER 6

1. *The Documents of Vatican II*, ed. by Abbott and Gallagher, pp. 662–63

2. Paul Tillich, *Christianity and the Encounter of the World Religions*, New York: Columbia University Press, 1963, pp. 57–58

3. Hendrik Kraemer, *The Christian Message in a Non-Christian World*, New York: Harper, 1938, pp. 108, 110, 418–19

4. Joseph M. Kitagawa in *New Frontiers of Christianity*, ed. by Ralph C. Raughley, Jr., New York: Association Press, 1962; pp. 168–73

5. Tillich, *Christianity and the Encounter of the World Religions*, pp. 54–59; for the reference to telos, p. 64

6. Ibid., p. 62

7. Arnold Toynbee, *Christianity among the Religions of the World*, New York: Scribner, 1957

CHAPTER 7

1. Beaver, *Ecumenical Beginnings*, chapters 1 and 2

2. Anderson, *To Advance the Gospel*, ed. by R. Pierce Beaver, introductory essay; Peter Beyerhaus and Henry Lefever, *The Responsible Church and the Foreign Mission*, Grand Rapids: Eerdmans, 1964, pp. 29–33

3. *Pan-Anglican Conference, 1908, Report*, vol. V, sec. D, "The Church's Mission in Non-Christian Lands," London: SPCK, 1908, D4 (e), p. 9

4. *World Missionary Conference, 1910*, 9 vols., Edinburgh: Oliphant, Anderson, and Ferrier, and New York: Revell, 1910, vol. II, p. 3

5. *Jerusalem Meeting of the International Missionary Council, 1928*, 8 vols., New York: I.M.C., 1928, vol. III, pp. 165–66

6. J. Merle Davis, *New Buildings on Old Foundations*, New York and London: I.M.C., 1945; also *The Economic and Social Environment of the Younger Churches*, London: Edinburgh House Press, 1939; *The Economic Basis of the Church*, vol. V of the *Madras Series*, New York: I.M.C., 1939

7. International Missionary Council, *The World Mission of the Church* (Madras Conference Report), London and New York: I.M.C., 1939, p. 26

8. Davis' books listed in note 6 give information on some of the churches

9. John L. Nevius, *The Planting and Development of Missionary Churches*, 4th ed., Grand Rapids: Baker, 1958; Charles A. Clark, *The Korean Church and the Nevius Methods*, New York: Revell, 1928; Beyerhaus and Lefever, *The Responsible Church*, pp. 90 ff

10. Roland Allen, *Missionary Methods, St. Paul's or Ours?*, London: R. Scott, 1912, latest ed., Grand Rapids: Eerdmans, 1962; *The Spontaneous Expansion of the Church*, 1st American ed., Grand Rapids: Eerdmans, 1964; *The Ministry of the Spirit*, Grand Rapids: Eerdmans, 1964

11. London: SCM Press, 1958

12. Loewen, numerous articles in *Practical Anthropology* from vol. 8, no. 6, November–December 1961, to the present; Dournes, *God Loves the Pagans*

13. Eugene A. Nida, "The Indigenous Churches in Latin America," in *Practical Anthropology*, vol. 8, no. 2, March–April 1961, pp. 99–105

14. William A. Smalley, "Cultural Implications of an Indigenous Church," *Practical Anthropology*, vol. 5, no. 2, March–April 1958, p. 51

15. Smalley, "Practical Problems," *PA*, same issue as note 14, p. 85

16. Loewen, "The Church: Indigenous and Ecumenical," *Practical Anthropology*, vol. 11, no. 6, November–December 1964, p. 243

17. Dournes, *God Loves the Pagans*, p. 181

CHAPTER 8

1. Wieser, *Planning for Mission*, see note 5

2. Despite the prevalence of complete devolution and disbanding of the field missions, some mission boards and societies operate as they did when founded seventy-five or a hundred years ago in the most authoritarian manner

3. See reports of two recent consultations listed in notes 7, ch. 4, and 3, ch. 5

4. Webster, *Local Church and World Mission*, pp. 68–69

CHAPTER 9

1. J. E. Lesslie Newbigin in Charles C. West and David M. Paton, *The Missionary Church in East and West*, London: SCM Press, 1959, p. 83

2. Webster, *Local Church and World Mission*, p. 21

3. London: Edinburgh House Press, 1964

4. Yves de Montcheuil, *Aspects of the Church*, tr. by Albert J. La Mothe, Jr., Chicago: Fides Publishers, 1955, pp. 190–91

5. Tokichi Ishii, *A Gentleman in Prison, with the Confession of Tokichi Ishii Written in Tokyo Prison*, tr. by Caroline Macdonald, New York: Doran, *ca.* 1922

6. Ibid., pp. 79, 82

7. Quoted in John Liggins, *The Great Value and Success of Foreign Missions*, New York: Baker and Taylor, *ca.* 1888, pp. 72–73

8. Loewen, "The Church among the Choco of Panama," *Practical Anthropology*, vol. 10, no. 3, May–June, 1963, pp. 97–108

9. Dournes, *God Loves the Pagans*, pp. 32, 203

10. Ibid., p. 200

Bibliography

Allen, Roland. *The Ministry of the Spirit,* Grand Rapids: Eerdmans, 1964
   Missionary Methods, St. Paul's or Ours?, Grand Rapids: Eerdmans, 1962
   Missionary Principles, Grand Rapids: Eerdmans, 1964
   Spontaneous Expansion of the Church, Grand Rapids: Eerdmans, 1962

Anderson, Rufus. *Foreign Missions: Their Relations and Claims,* New York: Scribner, 1869
   To Advance the Gospel, Selections from the Writings of Rufus Anderson, ed. by R. Pierce Beaver, Grand Rapids: Eerdmans, 1967

Beaver, R. Pierce. *All Loves Excelling. American Protestant Women in World Mission,* Grand Rapids: Eerdmans, 1968
   Ecumenical Beginnings in Protestant World Mission, a History of Comity, New York: Nelson, 1962

Envoys of Peace: The Peace Witness in the Christian World Mission, Grand Rapids: Eerdmans, 1964

Pioneers in Mission: The Early Missionary Ordination Sermons, Charges, and Instructions, Grand Rapids: Eerdmans, 1966

To Advance the Gospel: Selections from the Writings of Rufus Anderson, see Anderson above

Beyerhaus, Peter, and Henry Lefever. *The Responsible Church and the Foreign Mission,* Grand Rapids: Eerdmans, 1964

Carden, John. *The Ugly Missionary,* London: Highway Press, 1964

Davis, J. Merle. *New Buildings on Old Foundations,* New York and London: International Missionary Council, 1945

The Documents of Vatican II, ed. by Walter M. Abbott, S.J., gen. ed., and Msgr. Joseph Gallagher, tr. ed., New York: Guild Press, America Press, Association Press, 1966

Dodge, Ralph E. *The Unpopular Missionary,* Westwood, N.J.: Revell, 1964

Dournes, Jacques. *God Loves the Pagans. A Christian Mission on the Plateaux of Vietnam,* tr. by Rosemary Sheed, New York: Herder and Herder, 1966

East Asia Christian Conference. "Report of Consultation on Asian Missionaries, Bangkok, Feb. 18–22, 1964." mimeo.

International Missionary Council. *Jerusalem Meeting of the I.M.C., 1928,* 8 vols., New York and London: I.M.C., 1928

The World Mission of the Church, London and New York: I.M.C., 1938

Ishii, Tokichi. *A Gentleman in Prison,* tr. by Caroline Macdonald, New York: Doran, *ca.* 1922

Kraemer, Hendrik. *The Christian Message in a Non-Christian World,* New York: Harper, 1938

Loewen, Jacob A. Numerous articles, mostly about the Choco Indians, *Practical Anthropology,* vol. 8, no. 6, pp. 275–79;

vol. 9, no. 3, pp. 129–33; vol. 10, no. 3, pp. 97–108; vol. 11, no. 2, pp. 49–54; no. 3, pp. 97–104; no. 4, pp. 146–60; no. 5, pp. 173–203; no. 6, pp. 241–58; vol. 12, no. 2, pp. 49–62; no. 2, pp. 76–84; no. 3, pp. 97–106; no. 4, pp. 193–209; no. 6, pp. 250–80; vol. 13, no. 4, pp. 97–114; no. 5, pp. 213–26; no. 6, pp. 252–72; vol. 14, no. 2, pp. 49–72; no. 4, pp. 145–60; no. 5, pp. 173–208

Neill, Stephen. *The Unfinished Task*, London: Edinburgh House Press and Lutterworth Press, 1957

Nevius, John L. *The Planting and Development of Missionary Churches*, 4th. ed., Grand Rapids: Baker, 1958

Newbigin, Lesslie. *One Body, One Gospel, One World: The Christian Mission Today*, New York and London: International Missionary Council, 1958

Orchard, Ronald K. *Missions in a Time of Testing*, Philadelphia: Westminster Press, 1964
Out of Every Nation. A Discussion of the Internationalization of Mission, London: SCM Press, 1959

Practical Anthropology, vols. 8–14, 1961–67

Sargent, Douglas N. *The Making of a Missionary*, London: Hodder & Stoughton, 1960

Scherer, James A. *Missionary, Go Home!*, Englewood Cliffs, N.J.: Prentice-Hall, 1964

Speer, Robert E. *What Constitutes a Missionary Call?*, New York: Association Press, 1918. pamphlet

Tillich, Paul. *Christianity and the Encounter of World Religions*, New York: Columbia University Press, 1957

Toynbee, Arnold. *Christianity among the Religions of the World*, New York: Scribner, 1957

van Leeuwen, Arend Th. *Christianity in World History*, London: Edinburgh House Press, 1964

Webster, Douglas. *Into All the World*, London, S.P.C.K., 1959

Local Church and World Mission, New York: Seabury Press, 1964

Unchanging Mission, Philadelphia: Fortress Press, 1965

What Is a Missionary?, London: Highway Press, 1958

West, Charles C., and David M. Paton. *The Missionary Church in East and West,* London: SCM Press, 1959

Wieser, Thomas, ed. *Planning for Mission: Working Papers on the New Quest for Missionary Communities,* New York: U. S. Conference for the World Council of Churches, 1966

World Council of Churches, Commission on World Mission and Evangelism. *Joint Action for Mission,* Geneva: W.C.C., 1962. pamphlet

Statement from a Consultation on the Preparation of Missionaries, Toronto, 1963, Geneva and New York: W.C.C., 1963. pamphlet

Witness in Six Continents, London: Edinburgh House Press, 1964

ADDITIONAL READING

The reader is referred to two other books by Douglas Webster: *What Is Evangelism?*, London: Highway Press, 3d ed., 1964, and *Yes to Mission*, New York: Seabury Press, 1966. The following books by Max Warren will be provocative of thought: *Challenge and Response*, New York: Morehouse-Barlow, 1959; *The Christian Imperative*, New York: Scribner, 1955; *The Christian Mission*, London: SCM Press, 1951; *Letters on Purpose*, London: Highway Press, 1963; *Perspectives on Mission*, London: Hodder & Stoughton, 1964; and *Tell in the Wilderness*, London: Highway Press, 1959. For a quick overall glance at the transition stage of world mission: R. Pierce Beaver, *From Missions to Mission*, New York: Association Press, 1964.